Blessings
in the Rain

90 Days of Encouragement
through the Storm

Lisa DeVinney

Cover photo is by the author, Lisa DeVinney.

Copyright 2020	Lisa DeVinney
ISBN:	**978-1-71687-965-4**
Publisher	Cook Communication
Published	June, 2020
Language	English
Binding	Perfect-bound Paperback
Interior Ink	Black & white
Cover Ink	Full colour
Dimensions	6 inches wide x 9 inches tall

Dedication

To my sweet friend, Donna Dean Bartz, and her husband John who have inspired this book through their courage and steadfast faith. #BlessingsInTheRain

And to my Heavenly Father, for the gifts He has given and the promise "that he who began a good work in you will carry it on to completion until the day of Christ Jesus." Philippians 1:6 NIV.

With love,
Lisa

Introduction

I'm wearing a new wristband. It's white with a fading-blue message that reads *#BlessingsInTheRain*. My friend John Bartz wears one too. So does my husband, and perhaps hundreds or more others who know and love Donna Dean Bartz.

Donna is a follower of Jesus, a third grade teacher, pastor's wife to John, mom of two grown children. And I get to call her friend.

In January of 2019, Donna took on a new role – cancer warrior. With no history of smoking or cancer in the family, she was diagnosed with "non-small cell" lung cancer. And before they found it, the cancer had already spread to her bones.

It's never a good time to hear the word "cancer." But with two family weddings coming up quickly, and so many details still to be worked out, it seemed the timing couldn't be worse.

And so, the treatments began. Followed by infections. And surgeries. Successes and setbacks. The many ups and downs that always accompany such trials. But through it all, one thing seems to remain constant – Donna's joy. She and John determined early on to find the joy in each day, the new miracles and mercies God was sending along the way - their blessings in the rain.

I've had a few friends ask when I would be putting another devotional book together. And honestly, I thought I was done. But watching Donna's courageous and joy-filled battle has inspired me to do just one more. Its format is a bit different from the others. I've included some Questions to Consider, some Room for Reflection, and Space for Grace - where you can share your own thoughts, prayers and blessings.

My prayer is that Donna's story, along with these Scriptures, poems, and your own responses will encourage and inspire you to find your own BlessingsInTheRain.

~

*"I will send down
showers in season;
there will be*
**showers
of blessing**.*"*

Ezekiel 34:26b NIV

~

~ *Day 1* ~
Standing in the Rain With Jesus

One of my favorite names for Jesus is Immanuel, "God *with* us." He walked this Earth with the New Testament believers. And He is with us, still. So in the midst of your storm remember…you are not alone. Even in the raindrops, there are blessings with Jesus by your side.

~

"I have called you by name; you are mine. When you go through deep waters, I will be with you." Isaiah 43:1b-2a NLT

~

Oh, what a friend I have in my dear Savior.
Though He has not seen fit to take my pain,
Instead my Lord has drawn me ever closer
To taste the sweetness in the falling rain.

For even rain brings with it special blessings;
A spirit-richness I'd not known before.
So I'll stand here, out in the rain with Jesus;
And look beyond to Heaven's sunny shore.

And as He takes me by the hand, I'll smile
Just knowing He will stay close by my side.
For He has promised He will never leave me;
And whispers softly in my ear, "Abide."

So with whatever breath that still remains,
I'll praise Him, as we're standing in the rain.

*"I will send down showers in season; there **will** be showers of blessing." Ezekiel 34:26b NIV*

~ Space for Grace ~

~ *Day 2* ~
Wakened for Sunrise

"...and the sheep recognize his voice and come to him." John 10:3a NLT

~

The room was nearly pitch-black; my pillow, soft and comfy. As I quietly rolled over to go back to sleep, out of the darkness I heard these inviting words, "Come and see!"

We were on vacation, and our hotel room faced east, overlooking a lake. Each night I thought about setting an alarm for sunrise, but didn't.

It was our last morning of vacation when I woke to that darkened room and the silent invitation…"Come and see!" And though half-asleep, I recognized the Voice. So I slipped out from under the covers, peeked through the curtains, and nearly cried. It was spectacular! God had wakened me just in time for His glorious sunrise; and I could only stand there absolutely stunned by its beauty. His beauty!

And to think what I would've missed had I simply ignored that voice and gone back to sleep. I learned a few things that rosy morning. Sometimes when God calls, it requires moving outside our comfort zone, often into an uncomfortable darkness. Sometimes it will feel like we can't see the way ahead. But ultimately, answering His call is always worth the sacrifice. So when I sense an inviting nudge from my sweet Heavenly Father, I should always and happily say, "Yes!"

~

God wakened me for sunrise.
'Twas beautiful indeed,
With fiery pinks and oranges
Far as the eye could see.

The sun was not yet high enough
For me to see its face.
But there a beam of blushing light
Rose radiant in its place.

Blessings in the Rain

And only moments later
The sun itself appeared,
Its red-orange figure rising
So warm, and bright, and clear;

Much like my radiant Savior
Whose face I may not see.
But as His light and warmth surround,
I know He's close to me.

And in time He reveals His face,
Declaring His great love;
Assuring me I'm just the one
That He's been thinking of.

"Then your light will break forth like the dawn,
and your healing will quickly appear;
then your righteousness will go before you,
and the glory of the Lord will be your rear guard."
Isaiah 58:8 NIV

~ Questions to Consider ~

Have you ever sensed that God was speaking to you? If so, did you listen to Him? or convince yourself that you had only imagined it? and was it through His Word, or some other way?

~ Room for Reflection ~

Consider for a moment how amazing it is that the God of the universe invites us to know Him through His Word, and even recognize His voice!

"what are mere mortals that you should think about them,
human beings that you should care for them?" Psalm 8:4 NLT

~ *Day 3* ~
A Bridge to Courage

Shortly after my husband Dan and I began sensing God's call to full time ministry, I had a challenging dream. I was standing at the edge of a wide ravine. A rope bridge with wooden planks spanned the expanse from one side to the other. And in the gorge far below, a raging river had cut a path toward the horizon. I'm a little afraid of heights, and don't relish the idea of drowning. So I thought I would just stay put right where I was, safe on my side of the bridge. I thought I was alone there. But as I watched the water rush below me, I heard someone next to me say two simple words. "Step out!" I never saw the person who spoke, but sensed it was an angel. Then before I could take a single step forward onto the bridge, or backward to what seemed a safer place, I woke up from my dream.

I knew at once God was challenging me to consider whether I would trust Him, and take that step toward ministry; or pull back, away from the unknown. And I could not get that bridge or those words out of my mind.

Step out!

~

Today I pray for courage –
That I might not draw back;
That I might not heed Satan's voice,
Or yield to his attack.

But that in faith I'd step up
To what You've planned for me,
Take hold of Your intentions
For what is yet to be.

I pray that fear be vanquished,
For it is not of You;
And that the courage You supply
Will help me make it through.

Blessings in the Rain

For You know Your plans for me;
And I must trust Your grace.
You've built a bridge through faithfulness;
You've laid each plank in place.

It's up to me to *step out* –
To cross that bridge You laid;
And not let fear constrain me,
Or crush the plans You've made.

Then as I cross the bridge, I'll
Add planks of gratitude –
Reminders of how I've been blessed
By trusting, Lord, in You.

"Haven't I commanded you:
be strong and courageous? Do not be afraid or discouraged,
for the Lord your God is with you wherever you go."
Joshua 1:9 HCSB

~ Questions to Consider ~

Is God challenging you to do something courageous, stepping outside your comfort zone?

Can you recall examples of God's past faithfulness in your life?

~ Space for Grace ~

What planks of gratitude can you add to the bridge today?

~ *Day 4* ~
Teachable

"Show me Your ways, O Lord; Teach me Your paths.
Lead me in Your truth and teach me,
For You are the God of my salvation..."
Psalm 25:4-5a NKJV

~

Have you heard the expression about old dogs and new tricks? Tradition has it that as we get older, we tend to be less teachable. We get set in our ways; comfortable in our familiar surroundings. And we just don't really like change.

I don't know about you; but it sure is true for me!

But God's desire for us is that we remain teachable throughout our lives. We never grow too old to experience a little more of God's grace, His love or His mercy. And oftentimes we learn those graces best in a classroom of trial and testing. Will we trust Him enough to let Him teach in His way and time?

~

Step back; and let me do what I do best –
Work in your life to see that you are blessed.
Don't get discouraged when you cannot see
The answers to the things you've asked of Me.
For child, My ways and yours are not the same.
I'm orchestrating on a higher plane.

And though you may feel helpless, that's okay.
In fact, it really is the only way
For Me to show my power and strength to you;
As you admit there's nothing you can do
But lean on Me. That's just the place to start!
For I can take a humble, searching heart
And teach you what it is to know My grace.
My classroom is your quiet, secret place.

Blessings in the Rain

"Who is the man that fears the LORD?
Him shall He teach in the way He chooses."
Psalm 25:12 NKJV

~ Questions to Consider ~

What kind of pupil do you tend to be? Would you describe yourself as teachable? Do you feel you still have something to learn?

Are you willing to allow God to teach you "in the way He chooses?"

~ Room for Reflection ~

*What is God teaching **you** today?*

~ Space for Grace ~

~ *Day 5* ~
An On-Time God

Have you been praying about someone or something that's been weighing heavily on your heart, but it just doesn't seem like God is answering?

It can be so hard to wait. To wait for God's answer. To wait on His timing. But He has had lots of practice getting things done just the right way, in just the right time. No matter how it feels right now, He IS an on-time God.

Here's what He says in His Word:

> *"Though it tarries, wait for it;*
> *Because it will surely come,*
> *It will not tarry."*
> *Habakkuk 2:3 NKJV*

~

God's right on time, as always,
To do a work in me;
Sending the touch I needed most,
Or clearing eyes to see

That He'd already been at work
Before I stopped to pray.
I'd just not recognized His hand,
Or sensed His gentle way.

Oh thank You, Lord, for showing me
Your time and way are best;
And that You are an on-time God
Who makes sure I am blessed.

~

"To everything there is a season,
A time for every purpose under heaven."
Ecclesiastes 3:1 NKJV

~ Questions to Consider ~

How do you feel about the word "patience?" Does it make you anxious? Frustrated?

What are you waiting for God to do in your life today?

Have you ever been so frustrated waiting for God to answer your prayers that you took matters into your own hands? If so, did it turn out well? Or did you wish you had waited on God?

~Room for Reflection ~

Is what you're waiting for something that God has promised in His Word that He will do? If it is, you can be sure He will answer in the very best way and time.

~ Space for Grace ~

Why not take a moment to thank God again for His faithfulness in answering your prayers.

~ *Day 6* ~
It's Grace!

What are you running from today, my friend? Responsibilities that seem beyond your capabilities? Circumstances that seem overwhelming? People who are asking more of you than you feel you can give?

Author and speaker, Ann Voskamp, shares this encouraging thought:

> *"Whatever is chasing you –*
> *no matter what it looks like –*
> *it's grace."*[1] ~ Ann Voskamp

> ~

> *"Surely your goodness and unfailing love*
> *will **pursue** me*
> *all the days of my life…"*
> *Psalm 23:6a NLT*

~

We're being chased
by grace.
No matter what it looks like,
regardless of its face,
It's grace.

Grace in hidden
shape and size,
when looking through
the Father's eyes,
is still grace.

Blessings in the Rain

The sun, the rain,
the joy, the pain –
the end result
is all the same
for all is grace.

So whatever
the Father brings,
it is His best –
He knows all things.
And ALL is grace.

"And grace isn't what makes us feel good:
grace is all that makes us more like Jesus."[2]
~ Ann Voskamp

~ Questions to Consider ~

God is good, all the time. And He has promised to work everything out for our good (Romans 8:28). But sometimes the "good" things, the grace He brings into our lives, doesn't feel so good. When was the last time God's grace felt more like a trial?

~ Room for Reflection ~

Looking back, can you now see that trial as God's grace pursuing you?

~ Space for Grace ~

Can you thank God, even for the hard grace in your life?

~ *Day 7* ~
Though I Can't See It Yet

Imagine with me that you've been anxious about your future, struggling to figure out your next step – where you're supposed to go, what you're supposed to do. How are you supposed to move forward if you can't see the way?

Then picture this – Jesus comes alongside you, puts one arm lovingly around your shoulder, and stretches the other arm out in front of you, His finger pointing…directing your gaze toward the horizon. He seems to have His eyes fixed on something He can clearly see. But as you crane your neck and squint your eyes, you're still not able to see anything but empty space on the horizon. And yet Jesus seems so sure. So confident. So ready for you to take that first step.

Will you trust Him? Will you have peace knowing that He has a plan for your future, and that it's good? That's His promise, you know…

~

Lord, what am I supposed to see
With You standing here next to me;
And pointing with Your arm outstretched
Toward something that I can't see yet?

I know You have a plan in mind;
That in Your way, and in Your time,
It will be just as You have planned.
But right now, I don't understand.

So Lord, I'll take Your word by faith.
I'll trust Your guidance,
Seek Your face.
And when **You're** ready, I will see
The plans that You've prepared for me.

~

Blessings in the Rain

"For I know the plans I have for you,' declares the Lord,
'plans to prosper you and not to harm you,
plans to give you hope and a future.'"
Jeremiah 29:11 NIV

~ Questions to Consider ~

As a child, did you ever play a game where you were blindfolded and had to follow someone's directions, or try to find your way on your own? Was it fun? Or stressful?

Do you ever feel that way now? You know you need to take a step in a new direction but just can't see the way clearly? Or don't really know where you're headed?

~ Room for Reflection ~

In Psalm 57:7(NLT), David says, "My heart is confident in you, O God; my heart is confident." Can you move forward with confidence? Do you feel Jesus by your side, pointing the way? What's holding you back?

If you're not sure which direction to go, have you asked God to simply reveal the next little step? His desire is for us to be obedient, and we can't do that without knowing His will. But often He shows us just one step at a time, as the Lamp to our feet (Psalm 119:105). Ask Him to reveal that step to you. Time in His Word is a great place to start! And here's an extra clue – try Matthew 6:33. What is God asking you to do next?

Blessings in the Rain

~ *Day 8* ~
Every Sigh

Have you ever been so frustrated, hurt, discouraged, or in such deep despair that you couldn't even find the words to pray? If that's you today, God wants you to know that He hears your heart. And He wants to encourage you with these words...

~

"Likewise the Spirit helps us in our weakness.
For we do not know what to pray for as we ought,
but the Spirit himself intercedes for us
with groanings too deep for words."
Romans 8:26 ESV

~

Even when I cannot breathe the words,
He hears my sigh.
He knows exactly what I'm feeling;
Hears my inner cry.

And He wants nothing more than that I'd
Come to Him in prayer,
To lay my burdens at His feet,
And cast on Him my care.

He's always waiting for me with
His arms held open wide.
He whispers to me softly as
He draws me to His side.

And I know I don't even have
To speak aloud the words.
For my sweet Father knows my heart,
And every sigh is heard.

~

Blessings in the Rain

"You have heard my voice:
"Do not hide Your ear from my sighing,
from my cry for help."
Lamentations 3:56 NKJV

~ Questions to Consider ~

Is there something so heavy, so deep on your heart today that you don't even know where to begin talking with God about it?

Do you have the Holy Spirit within you to pray with and for you in those times? If you've trusted in Jesus Christ as your Lord and Savior, the Spirit is there.

If you don't know what it means to have the Holy Spirit living within you, please go to the final page of this book, and look for "Giving Your Life to Jesus."

~ Room for Reflection ~

Nothing you say or even think will ever take God by surprise. So don't ever feel like you have to hold back when pouring out your heart to Him. But also be assured that when you're too sad, discouraged, or despondent to put those thoughts into words of prayer, that's when His Spirit will be there to do the praying for you; and He always knows just .what to say.

~ Space for Grace ~

~ *Day 9* ~
Moon Flowers

I've never had much of a green thumb. So when we moved to Pennsylvania, and all sorts of mysterious plants began popping up all over our yard that first Spring, I was so excited! We had raspberries, blueberries, asparagus, rhubarb, peonies, mint… and several plants I'd never seen before. So each day, I would post pictures of our mystery vegetation on Facebook, hoping someone with a little greener thumb might recognize them. I was delighted to learn that our lawn was teeming with Ipomoea alba, affectionately known as "moon flowers."

~

Did you know there's a flower
That only blooms at night?
It waits until the sun goes down,
And there is little light.

Then as the darkness settles in
Beneath the rising moon,
It then opens so gracefully
Its luminescent bloom.

The pure-white of its blossom
And trumpet-like design
Make it appear, at twilight,
To glow along its vine.

A beauty to behold! Yet
Needs darkness to be seen.
How like our own refinement
When trials intervene.

For there are things we only learn
When in our darkest night,
As grace then fully blossoms in
The glow of God's Sonlight.

Blessings in the Rain

So may we not despair when
That darkness closes in.
Perhaps something will blossom
Before the trial's end.

For God has sweetly promised
There's purpose in each test.
And sometimes we need darkness,
To see we're truly blessed.

"...but we also rejoice in our afflictions,
because we know that affliction produces endurance,
endurance produces proven character,
and proven character produces hope.
This hope will not disappoint us,
because God's love has been poured out in our hearts
through the Holy Spirit who was given to us."
Romans 5:3-5 HCSB

~ Questions to Consider ~

Has God recently used a season of darkness to grow something new,
something beautiful in you?

Were you able to recognize the bright spots in the midst of the darkness?
Or did you need a little time and distance to see how God worked it out for
your good?

~Room for Reflection ~

If you find yourself in a dark place right now, can you trust God to walk
through that time with you, and use it to grow greater faith and strength in
you?

~ *Day 10* ~
And Yet We Praise

*"Be thankful in **all** circumstances,*
for this is God's will for you
who belong to Christ Jesus."
1 Thessalonians 5:18 NLT

~

It's natural to be thankful for things we like, things that feel good and bring us joy. But what about sickness, separation, suffering, loss… can we be thankful in those circumstances, too?

~

We do not understand, and yet we praise You.
We may not see Your plan, but still we praise You!
For You have shown Yourself worthy of praise;
We know You're working still in wondrous ways.

And so, though we can't see the end, we trust You.
We know Your blessings You will send. We trust You!
For You have shown Yourself faithful and true.
How could You do ought else but see us through?

For You are still our Father, and we love You.
We kneel before Your altar, Lord; we love You!
So in our trials, Lord, be glorified.
Let us forever in Your will abide.

And let our hearts be filled with gratitude;
Rejoicing, as we lift our praise to You!

~

Blessings in the Rain

"The LORD is my strength and my shield;
My heart trusted in Him, and I am helped;
Therefore my heart greatly rejoices,
And with my song I will praise Him."
Psalm 28:7 NKJV

~ Questions to Consider ~

What are you praising God for today?

What is currently going on in your life that it's hard to be thankful for?

~ Room for Reflection ~

Can you recall any passages of Scripture that might help you be thankful,
even in difficult circumstances? Here's one to get you started:

"Dear brothers and sisters, when troubles of any kind come your way,
consider it an opportunity for great joy. For you know that when your
faith is tested, your endurance has a chance to grow.
So let it grow, for when your endurance is fully developed,
you will be perfect and complete, needing nothing." James 1:2-4 NLT

~ Space for Grace ~

~ Day 11 ~
Just Sittin'

"...Mary, sat at the Lord's feet, listening to what he taught.
'There is only one thing worth being concerned about.
Mary has discovered it, and it will not be taken away from her.'"
Luke 10:39, 42 NLT

~

A friend recently asked this question: When was the last time you just **be'd**? We're all so busy *doing.* And often those things we're doing are good things. But we're called human "**be**ings," not human "doings." God knows we need to ***Be** still, and know that [He is] God!" (Psalm 46:10a)*

Mary of Bethany gave us a great example to follow. Maybe we could all take just a moment to *be* with Jesus today.

~

I'm sittin' here with Jesus,
And lettin' love sink in.
I think I'll stay awhile,
Just listenin' to Him.

He tells me that He loves me,
And that I am His own;
That since His Spirit's with me,
I'll never be alone.

He brings to mind His promises
That He'll supply my need;
And tells me when I'm praying,
He's there to intercede.

And when He finds me weary,
He knows just what to do.
He wraps His arms around me,
And says, "I'll see you through."

Blessings in the Rain

So if you find me sittin',
You'll know just why I'm there –
I'm listenin' to Jesus,
And spendin' time in prayer.

Friend, if you'd like to join me,
What blessings are in store!
For Jesus' arms are plenty wide
To make room for one more.

~

"Come to me, all you who are weary and burdened,
and I will give you rest.
Take my yoke upon you and learn from me,
for I am gentle and humble in heart,
and you will find rest for your souls."
Matthew 11:28-29 NIV

~ Room for Reflection ~

When was the last time you simply sat quietly at Jesus feet, and just be'd?
There's no time like the present...

Share some thoughts that came to mind as you spent time just sittin' with
Jesus.

~ Day 12 ~
He Is...

*"If we're willing, God is our song when we are happy,
our escape when we are tempted, our hope when we're despairing,
our joy in tribulation, our strength in weakness,
and our immortality in dying."[3]*
- Beth Moore

~

*"Oh give thanks to the Lord, for **he is** good,
for his steadfast love endures forever!
Let the redeemed of the Lord say so,"
Psalm 107:1-2a ESV*

~

He is...

My song when I am happy,
My hope when in despair,
My joy in tribulation,
My cure for every care.

He is my strength in weakness,
My sheltered place to hide;
The One I've put my trust in,
And in whom I abide.

In sorrow, He's my comfort;
When tempted, my escape.
He's every hope and blessing;
He's every breath I take.

And when, in death, I look up,
He then will be my Life.
For He is my Redeemer,
My Savior, Jesus Christ.

~

"let them continually say, 'The Lord be exalted...'"
Psalm 35:27b HCSB

~ Room for Reflection ~

Now it's your turn. Who is Jesus to you?

~ Space for Grace ~

Consider writing out a prayer of gratitude for all that Jesus is.

~ *Day 13* ~
Do You Know, Child…

Think back to when you were a child… Can you recall a time that your Daddy picked you up and carried you? Maybe you are fortunate enough to have a picture of yourself in his arms. That is how God wants us to picture Him – holding us lovingly and protectively in His arms. And *His* arms are strong enough that no matter how big we get, He will never stop carrying us.

~

My child
do you know that I carried you
when the waters
grew too deep
the flames too hot
the path too rough

That I carried you
when you were too weary to walk
too sick to even stand
too broken to go on

My child
do you know that I carried you
though you squirmed to be free
though you stiffened your arms
to push away from Me

My child
do you know
that I carried you

That I carry you still…

~

Blessings in the Rain

*"And you saw in the wilderness how the Lord your God
carried you as a man carries his son all along the way you traveled
until you reached this place."
Deuteronomy 1:31 HCSB*

~ Questions to Consider ~

*What are you going through right now that makes it hard to stand on your
own?*

*Is it difficult for you to admit that you sometimes need someone else to
carry you? If so, why?*

~ Room for Reflection ~

*Can you think of times in the past that God has likely carried you
through? Did you realize it at the time?*

~Space for Grace ~

*Take a moment to thank your Heavenly Father for those times He picked
you up and carried you in His strong and capable arms.*

~ *Day 14* ~
Getting Through the Anguish

Does it seem as if your plans and dreams been reduced to a heap of ashes?
Does it feel like circumstances have left you beyond hope? I want to
encourage you to remember you're not alone, and whatever you're going
through is not without a purpose. Keep trusting that our good and gracious
Father has a plan, and it's to prosper, not harm you.

~

"For I know the plans I have for you,' declares the Lord,
'plans to prosper you and not to harm you,
plans to give you hope and a future.'"
Jeremiah 29:11 NIV

~

Give me patience through the anguish.
Give me eyes, oh Lord, to see
That my trials aren't meant to harm, but to
Perfect Yourself in me.

Give me joy amidst the anguish.
Give me grace to see it through.
Lift my eyes up from my circumstance,
To gaze, instead, on You.

Then remind me, Lord, that everything
That comes from You is good.
And help me, Lord, regardless,
To be thankful, as I should.

For You make even ashes
Turn to beauty, in Your time.
That's why, with joy, I place my hand
Securely, Lord, in Thine.

~

Blessings in the Rain

"The Spirit of the Lord God is on Me…
He has sent Me to heal the brokenhearted,
to proclaim liberty to the captives
and freedom to the prisoners;
to proclaim the year of the Lord's favor,
and the day of our God's vengeance;
to comfort all who mourn,
to provide for those who mourn in Zion;
to give them a crown of beauty instead of ashes…"
Isaiah 61:1-3 HCSB

~ Questions to Consider ~

Do you find yourself in any of the circumstances above: brokenhearted, imprisoned by sickness, fear, anxiety, bound by unseen chains, mourning a deep loss?

What circumstances brought you to that place?

~ Room for Reflection ~

*Do you believe that God is able and wanting to proclaim His favor and freedom **for you**? That He can exchange beauty for your ashes?*

~ Space for Grace ~

Thank Him today for His good plan for you. And let Him know that You trust Him to make something beautiful from your life!

~ *Day 15* ~
He's Able...Right There!

I vividly remember the day my friend spoke these words. We were sitting across the table from each other at Bible study, and she had been describing some difficult circumstances she had just walked through. With her head down, she shared the heartbreak. The pain. The frustration. But then she looked up at each of us gathered round the table. And with the sweetest smile, and twinkle of real joy in her crinkling eyes, she reminded us that no matter where we are – whether it's on the mountaintop, or in the lowest valley, in the midst of our storm, the height of our pain, the depth of our loneliness, the edge of our grief –

"God is able...right there!" (Janet Morsellino)

~

God's able on the mountaintop,
And in the valley low.
He's able when the stormy seas
Are tossing to and fro.

He's able in the darkest night,
And through the longest day.
He's able on the hardest path,
And as the seasons change.

He's able even in those times
We think we've strayed too far.
No matter where you've gone, my friend,
He's able, where you are.

~

"And God is able to bless you abundantly,
so that in all things at all times,
having all that you need,
you will abound in every good work."
2 Corinthians 9:8 NIV

~

~ Questions to Consider ~

Have you ever felt like you were just too hurt, too damaged, too discouraged, too afraid, too far off for God to reach and help you? What circumstances took you there?

Have you ever believed you had done too much for God to ever be able to forgive and heal you?

Did you know, friend, that we just aren't that powerful? It is a lie from either your enemy Satan, or your own accusing heart. God says that nothing we can do will ever separate us from the love of God?
*If you doubt it, find **Romans chapter 8** and read all about God's love and plans for you.*

~ Room for Reflection ~

*In the space below, write out the first sentence of **Romans 8:38**.*

The apostle Paul was convinced of this truth! Are you?

Use the remaining space to make a list of things that can separate you from God's love, making Him unable to help you. (Notice I didn't leave any room because He IS able…right there, wherever you are.)

~ Day 16 ~
When God Says "No"

God invites us to come asking, seeking, knocking…believing that He is still a miracle worker. (Matthew 7:7) But sometimes it seems like we pray fervently, and get no answer at all. Or worse yet, we get an answer, and it's "No." Should we then conclude that God doesn't love us enough to give us what we want?

Maybe instead, we could conclude that our Heavenly Father loves us enough to say "no" to our request, just as our earthly parents sometimes do when it's for our own good.

~

If answers that I seek are not to be,
Then help me, all the more, to trust in Thee.
To trust Your grace to be sufficient for
The heartache and the pain that lie in store.
To trust Your peace to calm the raging storm.
To trust Your will, regardless of its form.

For Lord, I know Your will and way are best;
That I learn faith and patience with each test.
So grant me wisdom, Lord, and eyes to see
Your hand at work to lift and strengthen me.

~

" 'For my thoughts are not your thoughts,
neither are your ways my ways,'
declares the Lord."
Isaiah 55:8 NIV

~

~ Questions to Consider ~

Have you ever had to say "no" to your own child in order to protect them from something that would be harmful to them? Or because you had something even better planned for them?

How did they initially respond to your answer?

Can you remember a time when God said "No" to something you thought you desperately wanted or needed? What had you asked Him for?

Did He give you something else instead? And if so, did you recognize right away that it was better for you than what you had asked for?

~ Room for Reflection ~

God wants us to come to Him with our requests. (see Matthew 7:7) When God says, "No," does it discourage you from going to Him with other requests? If so, how can you keep that from happening?

~ Space for Grace ~

Consider thanking God right now for the "No's" in your life.

~ *Day 17* ~
Flying Sideways

Before moving to southern Pennsylvania, my family and I lived in the Mid-Hudson Valley of New York, just east of the Catskill Mountains. It was a major thoroughfare for geese as they migrated with the changing seasons. So I had many opportunities to watch and learn from them. On one particular morning, I remember some of the geese struggling against a crosswind, while others seemed completely unphased by it. And I found myself wondering whether winds like that could actually *help* the geese, if they knew how to make the most of them.

Then I remembered these encouraging words from the apostle Paul for when we are challenged by contrary winds in our own lives –

"We can rejoice, too, when we run into problems and trials, for we know that they help us develop endurance. And endurance develops strength of character, and character strengthens our confident hope of salvation."
Romans 5:3-4 NLT

~

I watched the geese fly overhead this morning
Just as they have the past several days;
But noticed with the steady south wind blowing,
That some were flying just a little sideways.

See, they were heading west, out toward the mountains;
The wind was pushing at them from the side.
And some of them seemed unaffected by it.
But others struggled 'gainst the windy tide.

Perhaps the geese who seemed to fly undaunted
Are those who've flown through stormy winds before;
And in them, learned to better use their own wings
To let the strong winds guide them as they soar.

Blessings in the Rain

The trials we face are never meant to crush us.
Our Heavenly Father knows just what we need.
And if He sends a crosswind, it's to guide us,
And help us, even better, to succeed.

If we just beat our wings against the tempest,
We'll be those flying sideways, worn and spent.
But if we learn to let the storm winds guide us,
Then even in them, we can be content.

And in time, we'll rise higher on the winds
As we learn they just guide us back to Him.

~

*"We are pressed on every side by troubles, but we are not crushed.
We are perplexed, but not driven to despair."
2 Corinthians 4:8 NLT*

~ Questions to Consider ~

What contrary winds are pushing you a little sideways today?

*When was the last time you faced a crosswind in your life? Do you feel
like it helped you grow spiritually in some way? If so, how?*

~Space for Grace ~

Do you trust God enough to thank Him for the crosswinds He sends?

~ *Day 18* ~
Come to Me, Child

I recently heard someone say that the burdens we continue to carry are like heavy suitcases with wheels that we insist on picking up, rather than using the wheels that were made to do the work for us. Jesus invites us to lay our heavy burdens on His strong, capable shoulders. In exchange, He asks us to share His yoke. But it turns out His is easy to bear, since He's doing most of the lifting.

His invitation is hard to resist…

> *"Come to me, all you who are weary and burdened,*
> *and I will give you rest."*
> *Matthew 11:28 NIV*

Come to Me, you who are weary;
Lay down your burdens and stress.
Find in Me comfort, and refuge,
Hope, and compassion, and rest.

I know you've been sorely tested,
Suffering anguish and pain.
Come, fix your eyes now upon Me;
I will restore you, again.

Lean on the strength of My shoulder;
Rest in the warmth of My love.
Be still, and know I am with you,
Giving sweet peace from above.

Just for a time, let the world go.
Be with Me here, in this place.
Come to Me, child; lay your head down.
And rest in the depth of My grace.

~

Blessings in the Rain

"Take my yoke upon you and learn from me,
for I am gentle and humble in heart,
and you will find rest for your souls.
For my yoke is easy and my burden is light."
Matthew 11:29-30 NIV

~ Questions to Consider ~

What heavy burden are you holding onto?

Why do we insist on carrying our burdens when Jesus invites us to give them to Him?

Do you believe that Jesus can be trusted to handle your cares and problems? Has He been faithful to do so in the past?

What burden have you given to Him that He has carried for you?

~ Room for Reflection ~

Have you been able to find true rest in giving your burdens to Jesus? If so, what did that feel like?

~ Space for Grace ~

Take a moment to thank Jesus for His gift of rest.

~ *Day 19* ~
Rivers in the Desert

Sometimes the word "new" can be scary. We get comfortable in our old way of doing things, in our familiar surroundings. And we would just as soon have things stay as they are. But we rarely grow when we stay in our snug, little boxes. And God is forever trying to stretch us and teach us, so we'll be more like Him. Often that requires a time of testing, a new direction. But oh the joy - when our time in the desert is eclipsed by the discovery of a new path through the wilderness… a new river springing up in that desert!

At the age of fifty, God called me into a brand new phase of life – stepping out from more than twenty years as a full time wife and mom into full time Christian ministry with my husband, on a college campus. Talk about scary! But now I wouldn't trade it for anything. And I'm learning not to fear the new, when Jesus is leading the way.

~

Lord, You have made a new way where
There was no way before,
Like rivers in the desert leading
Me to something more…

A spring here in the wilderness
Where barrenness once reigned.
But You've brought forth a miracle,
This desert to reclaim.

And You have called me here to see
This wonder You've begun,
A work in me You've promised to
Empower till it's done.

All You require of me is that
I'm willing to obey –
To be part of the miracle
That You've begun this day.

Blessings in the Rain

"Do not remember the past events,
pay no attention to things of old.
Look, I am about to do something new;
even now it is coming. Do you not see it?
Indeed, I will make a way in the wilderness,
rivers in the desert."
Isaiah 43:18-19 HCSB

~ Questions to Consider ~

Starting something new can be exciting. But it can be scary, too.
Have you sensed God calling you to something new? If so, what is He
asking you to do?

And if so, are you eagerly stepping forward onto the new path? Or is
something holding you back?

What might stop you from following God in a new direction?

~ Room for Reflection ~

Have you considered what blessings might be in store if you follow God in
a new direction? What rivers might you find waiting for you?

~ *Day 20* ~
Divine Indulgence

Do you ever wonder if God gets weary of our asking Him for things? Sometimes as parents, we grow tired of hearing our children asking for the same things over and over again. But when they ask for something that's good for them, and that we are able to provide, it is such a joy to be able to say "Yes" to them, and see the smile on their faces.

God is a good, good Father. And He delights in being able to say "Yes" to us, too. That's why, when our hearts are in tune with His, He invites us to ask Him for those very things that are also His desire for us.

~

"and God said, 'What do you want?
Ask, and I will give it to you!'" 1 Kings 3:5b NLT

~

As I kneel by my bed for time in prayer,
I feel my precious Father meet me there;
And in the silence hear Him softly say,
"You are My child; indulge yourself, today!

"Pour out your heart to Me; and in My name
Ask what you will. Our hearts are now the same.
And I desire to lavish upon you
Your heart's desire; as Fathers long to do."

Oh dare I, Lord, reveal what's on my heart?
I fear I wouldn't know just where to start.
And yet, I hear you say it, Lord, once more,
"Indulge yourself...see what I have in store."

Then overwhelmed that He would love me so,
I close my eyes and smile, for now I know
What I will ask; for now I plainly see –
Lord, I would have what You would have for me.

~

Blessings in the Rain

"Take delight in the Lord,
and he will give you the desires of your heart."
Psalm 37:4NIV

~ Questions to Consider ~

What are some of your hearts desires today?

Have you talked with God about them?

Do you believe that what you want and what God wants for you are the same?

How can you know if your desires are also His?

~ Room for Reflection ~

What was the last thing you asked God for that He said "Yes" to?

~ Space for Grace ~

Spend a few moments thanking God again for His goodness to you – the yes's and the no's.

~ *Day 21* ~
God's Master Plan

"Don't give me that 'all things work together for good' speech."
Have you ever heard someone, from deep in the pit of their frustration and despair, utter those words? I have.

When we're fighting a battle, words sometimes fall flat. We can almost grow immune to their strength. But the truth of Romans 8:28 is not diminished by use.

So maybe you're not in a place right now to receive the comfort this verse is intended to bring. But tuck it away safely, because when the storm finally passes, its power and truth will once again ring true…even for you.

~

When you're lost in the midst of a trial,
And there's nothing familiar in sight,
If the darkness is gathering round you,
And the storm clouds are hiding the light,

Just remember the Son's there to guide you,
Even when there's no path you can see.
He may only reveal the next small step.
Just keep walking with Him, faithfully.

Then one day, as the storm clouds have parted,
And the Son's once again shining through,
You will see that His masterful plan has
Worked out all things, together, for you.

~

"And we know that all things work together for good
to those who love God, to those who are the called
according to His purpose."
Romans 8:28 NKJV

~

Blessings in the Rain

~ Room for Reflection ~

List all the circumstances that God cannot work together for good –
(notice there is no space for anything)

~ Questions to Consider ~

What circumstances are you, or someone you know, going through that
make it hard to believe that God can work it ALL together for good?

Can you begin, even now, to think of ways God could use your current
struggle as a blessing for you or others?

Have there been times in your life where God has brought good out of
trials and suffering? What good resulted from it?

~ Space for Grace ~

Knowing God has promised to bring about good, even from hard times,
can you thank Him for any current difficulties you're going through?

~ *Day 22* ~
When Footprints Tell Only Half the Story

There's a very familiar story about a single set of footprints in the sand. It's an amazing story, and well worth reading. But this isn't *that* "Footprints." I wrote this one after spending a day at the beach with my family several years ago.

~

"...the kingdom of our God
and the authority of His Messiah
have now come, because the accuser
of our brothers has been thrown out:
the one who accuses them
before our God day and night."
Revelation 12:10 HCSB

~

Satan, that Accuser, stood
Before the Lord one day
To make a claim against God's child –
Said she'd wandered away.

He felt quite sure that he was right
From looking at the road,
And seeing only Jesus' prints…
No signs that she had followed.

But Jesus simply smiled
As He pointed down the lane.
And Satan's voice was silenced by
The scene that now was plain.

For in the distance he now saw
The one he'd thought was lost
Walking along the narrow way
While carrying her cross.

Blessings in the Rain

And with each careful step she took,
As she placed each foot down,
She stepped only into the prints
Already on the ground.

For she would only step where Jesus'
Feet had gone before.
She hadn't strayed. Instead she'd traced
The steps of her dear Lord.

And as the Devil turned away,
The Lord looked back again,
And smiled as her footprints fell
In perfect step with Him.

~ Questions to Consider ~

Did you know that Satan is able to go before God and accuse us of wrong-doing? Would he have anything to point out in your life?

Did you know that when Satan stands to accuse us, we also have a Defender, an Advocate? Who is our Defender?

"But if anyone does sin, we have an advocate with the Father— Jesus Christ the righteous one. He himself is the atoning sacrifice for our sins..." 1 John 2:1-2 CSB

~ Room for Reflection ~

Can you think of a verse that might help you to step in Jesus' footprints? Here's a suggestion: write out Galatians 5:22 in the space below.

~ *Day 23* ~
Greater Than My Feelings

Sometimes we just need to be reminded -

"God is greater than our feelings..." 1 John 3:20b NLT

~

When I am **afraid**...   *God is greater than my feelings.*
When I am **discouraged**...   *God is greater than my feelings.*
When I'm feeling **insecure**...   *God is greater than my feelings.*
When I feel **unprepared**...   *God is greater than my feelings.*
When I'm feeling **"less than"**...   *God is greater than my feelings.*
When I am **lonely**...   *God is greater than my feelings.*
When I'm feeling **shame**...   *God is greater than my feelings.*
When I feel **useless**...   *God is greater than my feelings.*
When I'm feeling **broken**...   *God is greater than my feelings.*
When my **heart aches**...   *God is greater than my feelings.*
When I'm feeling **bitter**...   *God is greater than my feelings.*
When I am **impatient**...   *God is greater than my feelings.*
When I am **angry**...   *God is greater than my feelings.*
When I'm **frustrated**.   *God is greater than my feelings.*
When I am **weary**...   *God is greater than my feelings.*
When I'm feeling **condemned**...   *God is greater than my feelings.*
When I feel I've been **betrayed**...   *God is greater than my feelings.*
When I'm feeling **rejected**...   *God is greater than my feelings.*
When I feel I've been **dismissed**...   *God is greater than my feelings.*
When I'm feeling **anxious**...   *God is greater than my feelings.*
When I feel **regret**...   *God is greater than my feelings.*
When I feel **unwelcome, uninvited, unnoticed**...
                                                God is greater than my feelings.

~

"But thanks be to God! He gives us the victory
through our Lord Jesus Christ."
1 Corinthians 15:57 NIV

~

~ Questions to Consider ~

What do you need to be reminded that God is greater than today?

Does the fact that God promises you victory in Jesus help you to overcome any of those feelings?

~ Room for Reflection ~

What other Bible promises can you claim when these feelings are overtaking you?

Try starting with Philippians 4:6-7. There's room to write it below.

~ *Day 24* ~
Who's in Your Control Tower?

I love to fly! Do you? I don't love waiting for parking lot shuttles, or going through security lines at the airports. But that moment when the nose of the plane goes up, and the wheels are no longer touching the ground… It's exhilarating!

But if you've ever been thousands of feet above the ground, and experienced a situation like the one described in today's devotion, it might impact the way you feel about flying.

~

They flew on a collision course.
The pilot didn't know,
Till the controller in the tower
Called to tell him so.

He quickly dropped in altitude.
His passengers were scared!
They'd seen no sign of danger, so
They'd been caught unprepared.

Compartments broke wide open.
Things flew about inside.
The passengers were frightened, screaming,
Fearing for their lives.

They had no way of knowing
That such a scary move
Was not, itself, the greatest danger.
It's what pulled them through.

And life is sometimes like that
When God is in control.
It seems the worst has happened
To rock us, heart and soul.

Blessings in the Rain

But God, in His omniscience,
Can see what lies ahead.
And rather than catastrophe
Allows a drop, instead.

Our limited perspective
Might lead to fear and doubt.
But we can trust God's will and way
Will always work things out.

So with Him in your tower,
Faith's always your best choice.
God knows just what He's doing. Trust!
And listen to His voice.

~

*"Trust in the Lord with all your heart,
and do not rely on your own understanding;
think about Him in all your ways,
and He will guide you on the right paths."
Proverbs 3:5-6 HCSB*

~ Room for Reflection ~

Sometimes God allows us to go through difficult, scary situations. And we wonder why? Have you ever wondered if that trial was necessary to spare you from something worse? We may not always learn the reasons why we go through trials. But we can be sure that God always has a really good reason.

~ Space for Grace ~

Perhaps now is a good time to thank God for trials that may have spared you, or those you love, some deeper pain or loss.

~ *Day 25* ~
He Knows

Just when you think no one really knows or understands what you're going through...

"God heard their groaning...and God knew."
Exodus 2:24-25 ESV

~

What are the things you need to know God knows, today?
What burdens do you carry as you kneel to pray?
Take comfort, friend, in knowing He already sees;
And He's right there beside you as you hit your knees.

And He not only knows, friend, but He also cares.
When you're deep in a trial, He's already there.
No one but Jesus truly knows your greatest need.
That's why His Spirit's there, my friend, to intercede.

He knows your need. He feels your pain. He cares for you.
So trust Him now; and see what, in His love, He'll do.
He's working out the best for you, just watch and see.
His blessings stretch from now into eternity.

But be prepared, my friend; sometimes His answers come
In ways you won't expect.   You'll wonder what He's done.
But in the end, you'll find your faith in Jesus grows
As He reminds you that He sees. He cares. He knows.

~

"Then the Lord said, 'I have surely seen the affliction of my people...
I know their sufferings, and I have come down to deliver them'"
Exodus 3:7-8a ESV

~

~ Questions to Consider ~

What are the things you need to know God knows, today? Maybe something you feel you can't share with anyone else?

Do you believe God really knows you personally, and cares about you? How do you know? Do you know where He has promised that in His Word?

~ Room for Reflection ~

Here are some verses to get you started. What do they tell you about how God feels about you?

1 Peter 5:7

Psalm 55:22

Psalm 121

Matthew 6:26-33

~ Space for Grace ~

Write a prayer thanking God for how well He loves and cares for you -

~ *Day 26* ~
You Are Not Alone

We have an enemy. He whispers to us to look down at our circumstances, and remain focused there. But we have a Shepherd and Savior who invites us to fix our eyes, instead, on Him. And when we do, we find that regardless of our circumstances, we are not alone. He is there to take us by the hand and lead us through.

~

"Do not be anxious about anything,
but in every situation, by prayer and petition,
with thanksgiving, present your requests to God.
And the peace of God, which transcends all understanding,
will guard your hearts and your minds in Christ Jesus."
Philippians 4:6-7 NIV

~

When you opened your eyes this morn,
Was it with anxious thoughts of what's ahead?
God's Word says not to worry, but
To cast all of your cares on Him, instead.

He may not change the circumstance,
For it may be a time for you to grow.
But He'll supply sufficient grace
And strength beyond yourself, so you will know

How much He loves and cares for you
Despite the trials that tend to weigh you down.
For trials make opportunities
To see God's awesome love and grace abound.

So as you start this brand new day,
Come cast those worries at your Father's throne.
And listen to Him whisper that
He's there for you, and you are not alone.

~

Blessings in the Rain

*"Cast all your anxiety on him
because he cares for you."*
1 Peter 5:7 NIV

~ Questions to Consider ~

*Have you ever felt, or do you maybe feel today, like you're facing a battle
all alone? What is that battle you're facing?*

*What steps does Philippians 4:6-7 recommend to keep our anxious
thoughts from overcoming us?*

~ Room for Reflection ~

*Are you familiar with the story of Peter walking on the water to Jesus?
(Matthew 14:22-33) What happened to Peter when he looked down at the
wind and waves?*

What happened when Peter began to sink? Was he alone on the waves?

~ Space for Grace ~

Take a moment to thank God that He is there to face the new day with you.

~ *Day 27* ~
Picking up the Pieces

Sometimes the storms we face come in dark clouds and raging winds.
Sometimes they come from a doctor with devastating news. Sometimes
they are deep inside and those around us only see the broken pieces. But
regardless of how *your* storm blows in, there is Someone there with you to
help gather the broken pieces, and restore your soul.

This poem was written following a tornado outbreak in Illinois and
Indiana in 2013. But it's just as true for whatever storm you're facing
today.

~

When storms are swirling round us, and
Our backs are to a wall,
When life is strewn in pieces and
There's little hope at all,

When all that's left are mem'ries and
We ask the question, "Why?"
Our Father leans in closely, for
He hears each plaintive cry.

He wraps His arms around us, whisp'ring
Words of hope and grace.
He sends His angels down to wipe
Each weary, tear-stained face.

And as He's promised, He'll be there
To heal and intercede,
Supplying for each broken heart
And every daunting need.

His timing will be perfect, for
That's just the God He is.
Sometimes we cannot see it but
The time and way are His.

Blessings in the Rain

And He works all things for our good,
When we're holding His hand.
So trust Him, even now; He'll give
The strength and grace to stand.

~

"And my God shall supply all your need
according to His riches in glory by Christ Jesus."
Philippians 4:19 NKJV

~ Questions to Consider ~

Have you ever felt like your life was so broken that you didn't even know
where all the pieces were, not to mention how to put them back together?
What circumstances have stormed through your life?

Do you still feel like there are pieces missing?
If so, do you believe God is able to put things back together?

What can you do to find peace in the process?

~ Room for Reflection ~

Tradition has it that in some parts of the world, broken vessels were
pieced back together with gold or other precious metals, making them
even more valuable than they were to begin with.
That's how God sees us – precious in His sight because we've been
mended with the most valuable substance available… the blood of Jesus.

~ *Day 28* ~
Something Other

What are you wishing and praying for? Health? Wealth? Relief from pain?
A change in circumstances? Something other than what you have or
where you are… something other than what God has provided? If so,
you're not alone. Seems so many of us are longing for that something
other…

~

Lord, give me something other
Than the toilsome trials I've seen;
Other than the wilderness
Where times are hard and lean.

I long for something other than
You've chosen to provide;
But find that in this longing I
Just can't be satisfied.

This "other" that you long for, child,
Is not within My plan.
My longing is that you'd accept
The gifts I have in hand;

And trust that what I've chosen always
Will be best for you.
You've seen it time and time again,
And know it to be true.

So have some faith, My child, and open
Hand and heart to see
That there's no other better than
The other that's from me.

~

Blessings in the Rain

"Let your conduct be without covetousness;
be content with such things as you have."
Hebrews 13:5a NKJV

~ Questions to Consider ~

What are your "others"? Those things you have been praying for that God has not provided?

Have you asked God if your desires and His are the same?

~ Room for Reflection ~

What is God teaching you about contentment?

~ Space for Grace ~

In the space below, list other things that God, in His wisdom and grace, has chosen to provide for you – things you didn't ask for, but now see are (or will be) a gift from Him.

~ *Day 29* ~
Perseverance

"His master replied, 'Well done, good and faithful servant!'"
Matthew 25:21 NIV

~

I'm longing to hear these very words someday from my Lord and Savior, Jesus Christ. But they will only come after a life of faithful perseverance. I can't say I'm longing for *that* part, because perseverance comes from "the testing of your faith" and "trials of many kinds." (James 1) And who wants to go through that? But oh…it will be so well worth it when we get to hear those words from Jesus Himself, *"Well done!"*

~

If we should choose to let them,
Our trials could rob us blind.
They try to steal our hope and joy,
And pillage peace of mind.

But friend, if on the other hand
We let God have His way,
He'll use those trials to bring us joy,
When we trust and obey.

For tests build perseverance;
Which, when its work's complete,
Fulfills in us a finished work
At Jesus' Mercy Seat.

And oh! the joy we'll find, there,
Embraced by God's dear Son
Who'll say those words we've longed to hear,
"Come rest, My child. Well done!"

~

Blessings in the Rain

"Consider it pure joy, my brothers and sisters,
whenever you face trials of many kinds,
because you know that the testing
of your faith produces perseverance.
Let perseverance finish its work so that you may be
mature and complete, not lacking anything."
James 1:2-4 NIV

~ Questions to Consider ~

*What feelings come to mind when you hear the words **trial,** and **testing**, and **perseverance**?*

Did your list include joy?

Have you ever been in the midst of a trial, or gotten to the end, and realized you had found joy in the process? How can that happen?

~ Room for Reflection ~

What is God teaching you in your current circumstances?

~ Space for Grace ~

Take some time today to be thankful, even in the trials – keeping in mind that we're to "give thanks in all circumstances; for this is God's will for you in Christ Jesus." 1 Thessalonians 5:18 NIV

~ *Day 30* ~
God Is For Me!

There may be times when you wonder if God has forgotten you, lost sight of you in the midst of the storm, or maybe that He just doesn't care enough about what you're going through. I'm here to remind you today, my friend, that regardless of your circumstances, regardless of how it may feel at the moment, God wants you to rest assured that He is on YOUR side, fighting for you!

~

"This I know: God is for me."
Psalm 56:9b HCSB

~

When circumstances bring me down,
When doubt and anxious fears abound,
When Satan's lies are all around
I simply must remember…God is for me.

And when the path I take is long,
My heart too heavy for a song,
When I don't know where I belong
It's then I must remember…God is for me.

If loneliness would steal the night,
As those I love are gone from sight,
And there's no one to hold me tight
I whisper to myself that God is for me.

Oh what a blessed thought is this…
That even in my faithlessness
The Spirit in me bears witness
To reassure my heart that God is for me.

~

"What then are we to say about these things?
If God is for us, who is against us?"
Romans 8:31 HCSB

~ Questions to Consider ~

If you had the opportunity to pick a team to support you through this life, and you could pick anyone in the Universe, who would be your #1 pick?

Would you pick Jesus? Why or why not? What do you think Jesus would bring to your team?

If you have given your life to Jesus, that means He picked you for His team, too! How does that make you feel?

~ Room for Reflection ~

How is your life different with Jesus on your team? How might it look without Him?

~ Space for Grace ~

*Consider writing a prayer thanking God for picking you, and also for demonstrating that He is **for you** -*

~ *Day 31* ~
Going His Way

"as narrow as the path may appear, I am going that way."
- Grace Pedulla Dillon, September 2015

~

I am not sharing the details of what led up to my friend Grace sharing this thought because each one who reads this will be on their own journey, walking a road that might perhaps look very different from hers, but at the same time feel very much the same. For her, it was a time of loss, grief, and sadness. But it was also a time to anticipate what her good Father might have in store. What might He have in store for you?

~

My world is closing in, Lord…
Just a narrow path I see.
But I will walk that way with You,
If you will walk with me.

It seems so narrow, Lord; at times
The thorns along the way
Leave wounds that bleed and scar, and yet
You soothe the pain away.

And sometimes, Lord, it leads through waters
Murky, rough, and deep;
Or up a rocky mountainside
That's harsh, and wild, and steep.

But since You're here to hold my hand,
I'll walk this path of grace,
Trusting that it's best for me,
And there's no better place;

For I have placed my hand in Yours;
It's all that I can do.
So though the path seems narrow, Lord,
I'll go that way with You.

Blessings in the Rain

"you will weep no more.
He will be gracious if you ask for help.
He will surely respond to the sound of your cries.
Though the Lord gave you adversity for food
and suffering for drink,
he will still be with you to teach you.
You will see your teacher with your own eyes.
Your own ears will hear him.
Right behind you a voice will say,
'This is the way you should go…'"
Isaiah 30:19-21 NLT

~ Questions to Consider ~

Is there any place you wouldn't go with Jesus?

What might keep you from going His way? Fear of the unknown? Fear because of what appears to lie ahead?

Do you feel like a narrower path is easier or harder to follow? Why?

Has God ever told you to go or not go a certain way? If so, how did He make that known?

~ Room for Reflection ~

Why would a Good Shepherd lead us on narrow, difficult paths?

~ *Day 32* ~
Beyond Understanding

It was a beautiful mid-March day – sunny and 75 degrees, almost unheard of in upstate New York, where late winter days were often dreary and cold. But this day was absolutely perfect. Until the phone rang. There had been an accident. My sweet friend's husband had taken advantage of the weather to get his motorcycle out on the road. The other driver never saw him. He never had a chance. And I stood there in stunned silence, not knowing how to help. What could I possibly say to bring comfort to this dear woman whose life had just been turned upside down?

I learned two important things that day. Sometimes there are no words. But whether we have the words or not, the peace of Christ can bridge even those sounds of silence.

These words came later that night, reminding us both that even in the worst of circumstances, God is still love; and He can still offer us a peace that doesn't make any sense to the human heart. But is very real, nonetheless.

~

There is a peace beyond all understanding,
A peace that's found in Christ, and Christ alone;
Not bound by circumstance or storms around me.
I find it in the quiet of His throne.

And in those moments when His peace eludes me,
The nights when I cry out to feel His love,
He reaches down and wraps His arms around me,
And tells me I'm the one He's thinking of.

Blessings in the Rain

I know, then, that He'll stay beside me always,
No matter how the storms of life may rage;
And that the tears I cry are not forgotten,
His own sweet hands will brush each one away.

Oh Lord, please rock me in Your arms tonight.
Only Your peace and love can make things right.

~

"Then you will experience God's peace,
which exceeds anything we can understand.
His peace will guard your hearts and minds
as you live in Christ Jesus."
Philippians 4:7 NLT

~

~ Questions to Consider ~

Has your world ever been rocked by circumstances that threatened to steal your peace, or that of someone you love? What were those circumstances?

Were you able to find peace in the midst of the storm?

~ Room for Reflection ~

Where can you look for lasting peace? If it's eluding you today, spend time meditating on these words from Jesus - "I am leaving you with a gift—peace of mind and heart. And the peace I give is a gift the world cannot give. So don't be troubled or afraid." John 14:27 NLT

~ *Day 33* ~
Dawn's Early Light

If you're currently walking through a dark valley, it may seem like the long-awaited dawn will never come. But take heart, my friend – the new morning with its fresh mercies will indeed come; and with it, a joy and peace that defy reason. Joy and peace that are found only in Christ.

~

"Weeping may last through the night,
but joy comes with the morning."
Psalm 30:5b NLT

~

The shadows of the night are fading fast;
The light of a new dawn is stealing in.
The earth will not turn back upon the past;
But forward to the new day it will spin.

The tears of sorrow's night will fall away,
Brushed gently by God's tender, healing hand;
As joy is ushered in with this new day
Which dawns upon the soul at His command.

The long, cold night of weeping is behind.
A day bathed in the Son now lies before.
And once again, His promises remind
Of blessings that the Father has in store.

~

"Great is his faithfulness;
his mercies begin afresh each morning."
Lamentations 3:23 NLT

~

~ Questions to Consider ~

Psalm 23:4 (NLT) says, "Even when I walk through the darkest valley, I will not be afraid, for you are close beside me. Your rod and your staff protect and comfort me."

Does it make it any easier to walk through dark valleys when you know you're not walking through them alone?

Who promises to be there with you?

How might the presence of God's rod and staff bring you comfort and protection in the darkness?

~ Space for Grace ~

If you're currently walking through one of those dark valleys, thank Jesus for walking there alongside you, and for the promise that there will be joy...soon.

Since God has promised new mercies for each morning, what new mercies have you seen today?

~ Day 34 ~
Muddy Waters

Are you afraid to step out when the path isn't easy to see? Sure would be nice if God would put up giant billboards saying, "This is where you should go, and what you should do..." But He doesn't often move that way. Instead, He invites us to step into muddy waters, and simply says, "Follow Me."

In the Old Testament, a man named Naaman had leprosy, with no hope of a cure. But the prophet Elisha told him that God would heal him if he would wash in the Jordan River. Now, there was nothing magical about the river. In fact, it was often quite muddy. So there was no logical reason why that water would cleanse him. But finally, he stepped into that muddy river. And that, my friend, is faith! And because of his faithful obedience, God healed him.

I can't tell you that God will always heal our diseases this side of Heaven. But I can tell you that if God calls us to do something that seems crazy, He will find a way to bless us for our obedience.

~

When God asks us to follow where He's leading,
Sometimes the way is crystal-clear to see.
But other times it's into muddy waters
That we must step, not knowing what will be.

And just because it's murky doesn't mean that
God's hand is any less strong to provide.
Sometimes He'll stir things up, Himself, just knowing
That it will bring us closer to His side.

Now Satan, too, might muddy-up the waters,
Hoping to stir up doubt, delay, and fear.
But when we know for sure that God is leading,
It will not matter if the way is clear.

Blessings in the Rain

Just one step at a time with our Way-Maker
Will ultimately bring us to the place
Of living out the calling placed upon us
As we pursue His joy, His peace, His grace.

So don't hold back just 'cause there's muddy water.
Just listen closer to the Shepherd's voice;
And follow close enough to catch His current.
Obedience is always the best choice.

~

*"So Naaman went down and dipped himself in the [muddy] Jordan
seven times, according to the command of the man of God.
Then his skin was restored... and he was clean."*
2 Kings 5:14 HCSB

~ Questions to Consider ~

*Is God asking you to step out into uncertain circumstances? What is He
asking you to do?*

*Are you typically quick to jump into new, muddy water? Or are you
usually more cautious and reluctant?*

~ Room for Reflection ~

*Would you **welcome** an invitation from God to step into muddy water if He
asked you today? Why or why not?*

~ *Day 35* ~
...This I Know

*"Jesus loves me! this I **know**"*[4]
- Anna B. Warner

Do you *know* beyond any shadow of a doubt that you are loved? If you grew up in Sunday School, you might have sung the words "Jesus loves me, this I know for the Bible tells me so." That means if you believe God's Word to be true, then you can count on the fact that there is always Someone who loves you more than you can even imagine. God does!

When circumstances are difficult, and it seems like God isn't doing anything about it, we are sometimes tempted to believe that perhaps God doesn't really love us after all. But know this, my friend – you **are** loved!

Here's a little taste of how God says He feels about you:

"Even before he made the world, God loved us and chose us...
God decided in advance to adopt us into his own family by bringing us
to himself through Jesus Christ. This is what he wanted to do,
and it gave him great pleasure."
Ephesians 1:4-5 NLT

~

Draw me in, Lord. Pull me closer
So I'll better hear
Your voice so sweet, so still and gentle,
Not just in my ear
But deep within my longing heart
Where Your own Spirit dwells.
For there I hear my Shepherd's voice –
How tenderly it tells
Me just how much You love me, Lord;
And who I am to You –
Not just another stubborn sheep
(Though yes, I am that, too);

Blessings in the Rain

But also Your beloved child,
In whom, Lord, you delight.
You take me up into Your arms,
And there You hold me tight
Until I feel that I am loved
Far more than I can know.
I smile way down deep within
Each time You tell me so.

~

"I have loved you with an everlasting love;
I have drawn you with unfailing kindness."
Jeremiah 31:3 NIV

~ Questions to Consider ~

God says He loves us. But how do we know? How has God demonstrated His love to us in the past?

Can you think of any Bible verses that talk about God showing us His love? I've included a couple to get you started – How did God demonstrate His love in each verse?

John 3:16

Romans 5:8

How has God demonstrated His love in your life recently?

~ Space for Grace ~

Thank God today for His love, and the way you've seen it in your own life.

~ *Day 36* ~
Empty Hands, Open Heart

Have you ever seen the picture of the little child standing in front of Jesus where He is kneeling with his hand outstretched, asking her to give Him the little teddy bear she's holding so close? Her head is down and her eyes are sad, as she is reluctant to lose what she holds so dear. But what she cannot see is that Jesus holds an even bigger and better teddy bear behind His back. He wants to give her His bear, knowing how delighted she would be. But in order to have Jesus' bear, she must let go of the old one.

It's such a clear and sweet picture of Jesus, and His good plans for us. We tend to cling to the familiar, to things to which we've formed an attachment. But God knows those things aren't always best for us. He asks us to lay them down so that our hands will be open to receive what He has for us. Are you ready to let go, and let God fill your empty hands with His gifts of grace?

~

"Listen to the sound of my pleading
when I cry to You for help,
when I lift up my hands
toward Your holy sanctuary."
Psalm 28:2 HCSB

~

See me lift them up, Lord,
My open, empty hands…
I'm ready to accept, now,
Your sovereign, loving plans.

My own I now surrender;
I'd held them oh, so tight.
And only now have realized
How futile was the fight.

Blessings in the Rain

I'll sacrifice them to You -
My hopes, and plans, and dreams.
And yield to Your direction,
No matter what it means.

For I know when I open
My heart and hands to You,
Whatever, Lord, You ask of me,
You're there to see me through.

~

"He gives us grace and glory.
The Lord will withhold no good thing
from those who do what is right."
Psalm 84:11 NLT

~ Questions to Consider ~

What are you holding onto that God has asked you to let go of?

What makes it so hard to let go?

~ Room for Reflection ~

What has God provided for you in the past that can help you trust Him in the future?

~ *Day 37* ~
The Rhythm of Grace

I grew up in a church denomination that, back in those days, didn't dance. Not ever. Not even at weddings. But times have changed; and a few years ago I went to a recital where ballerinas danced for Jesus. It was beautiful and worshipful.

Not long after that recital, a friend shared this verse from The Message. And it reminded me of those young ladies who had danced for and with Jesus. I expect there will be dancing in Heaven. Until then, I can use my imagination…and my words.

~

"Come to me. Get away with me
and you'll recover your life.
I'll show you how to take a real rest.
Walk with me and work with me—
watch how I do it.
Learn the unforced
rhythms of grace…"
Matthew 11:28-29 MSG

~

Beloved, do you see
God's outstretched hand?
He's inviting you to dance
to the unforced rhythms of grace
where arms swing wide
to reach the furthest soul
then pull in close
in an embrace that says
"I love you,
and you are Mine"

Blessings in the Rain

a dance that leaves
but one set of footprints
as you stand upon the
toes of Jesus
feeling Him move
learning His steps
listening to His heart
as you lean in close
to rest upon Him

a dance with
unexpected turns
each more full and free
yet always spinning you
back to the Lover of your soul
back to His arms
safe in His love
caught in the wonder
and unforced rhythm
of His grace

~ Room for Reflection ~

Can you imagine this being you, dancing in the arms of Jesus? How would that feel?

Do you think we have to wait until Heaven for this to be a reality? Or is His invitation for today?

~ *Day 38* ~
Brave

"Be Brave. And do not pray for the hard thing to go away.
But pray for a bravery to come that's bigger than the hard thing."[5]
- Ann Voskamp

~

"Be strong and very courageous."
Joshua 1:7a NIV

~

Be brave; not praying that the hardest
Things would go away,
But asking for the grace and strength
To face them, day by day.

God says it time, and time again
Within His holy Word:
"Be strong and be courageous!"
Let your heart, my friend, be stirred

With confidence in Father God,
In His trustworthy plan,
In His great love and mercy, and
The strength of His right hand.

For He won't call us to a place
Without meeting us there,
With His ear bent to listen as
We come to Him in prayer,

And step up to the challenge that,
With confidence, He gave.
He's promised us the victory.
It's time now to be brave.

~

"Have I not commanded you? Be strong and courageous.
Do not be afraid; do not be discouraged,
for the Lord your God will be with you wherever you go."
Joshua 1:9 NIV

~ Questions to Consider ~

What are you facing today that requires you to be brave?

What have you faced in the past that required you to be strong and courageous?

Did you find God to be faithful through that time? If so, how?

~ Room for Reflection ~

Do you think God ever has to be brave? In what circumstances?

Does it help you to know that He knows how you feel? Spend a few moments reflecting on this verse, and thanking God for the truth it reveals about Him –
"This High Priest of ours understands our weaknesses, for he faced all of the same testings we do, yet he did not sin. So let us come boldly to the throne of our gracious God. There we will receive his mercy, and we will find grace to help us when we need it most." Hebrews 4:15-16 NLT

~ *Day 39* ~
Holes to Heaven

Some years ago, I heard a speaker share that she has learned to see losses in her life not as gaping holes that could never be mended, but instead as places where God had torn the canopy, just a bit, to allow her glimpses into Heaven. Because with each loss, she experienced a little closer glimpse of Jesus' face as He drew ever nearer to walk her through the darkness.

If there are gaping holes or wounds in your life, Jesus means to use those for your good, too. If there's something still unmended, perhaps He wants to use it to give you a window to His grace and glory.

~

"The Lord gives, and the Lord takes away.
Blessed be the name of the Lord."
Job 1:21 CSB

~

Have you begun to doubt a God
Who's taken part of what has made you whole?
Have heartaches of the past left tears
That let the joy seep slowly from your soul?

What if those holes are places where
Our hearts could peer past all the hurt and pain
To catch a clearer glimpse of God,
If only for a moment's brief refrain.

For in that moment's glimpse, we see
A God of greater mercy, love, and grace
Than ever could we know had we
Not gone into that dark and lonely place.

So if, indeed, your life's canvas
Is riddled with the gaping tears of life,
Remember they are glimpses into
Joy to be revealed in Jesus Christ.

*"For I consider that the sufferings of this present time
are not worth comparing with the glory
that is going to be revealed to us."*
Romans 8:18 NKJV

~ Questions to Consider ~

What have you experienced in the past that has left what feels like gaping holes in your heart?

Has anything helped to mend those holes?

~ Room for Reflection ~

What if instead of sewing those holes closed, God wants to leave them open just a bit to give you a better glimpse of Himself, or an opening for Him to give you something new – not a replacement… but room for something more. Can you trust Him that much with your heart, believing He will do what's best for you? Romans 8:28 reminds us that He can do no less because He works it ALL for our good. Here's a little refresher –

*"And we know that all things work together for good
to those who love God, to those who are the called
according to His purpose."*
Romans 8:28 NKJV

~ *Day 40* ~
Worth It All

Rain, rain, go away! Have you ever sung those words? Are you singing them today? Without rain there would be no rainbows, a reminder of God's promised protection. Without rain, plants wouldn't grow and we wouldn't have the proper amount of oxygen in the air to breathe properly.

God could have created a world that would function without rain. And He could arrange things so we would function without pain. But He didn't. He chose what was best for us. And that includes allowing storms to pass through our lives.

I almost changed the verse for today. When I chose the order of poems for this book, I did so rather randomly, trusting God to place them where they would be needed most. And that meant the same verse came up twice in consecutive days – yesterday and today. I'm convinced it was no coincidence on His part. So if He did it just for you, then smile today knowing you were on His mind.

~

If suffering can bring me closer to You,
If I can know You better through the pain,
Then I will trust Your loving hand upon me,
Even when You choose to send the rain.

And though the rainy days seem dark and dreary,
I know that I will see the sun again;
For I have learned that You will only take me
To places, Lord, that You've already been.

And since You've gone before me, I can follow
Your footprints, which will guide each step of mine.
For I have learned Your lamp will light the pathway,
Though it may be just one step at a time.

Then when the storm has passed, the clouds have parted,
And I've come through with faith that's been renewed,
I'll know that it, indeed, was worth it all
To find a deeper love and trust in You.

~

*"For I consider that the sufferings of this present time
are not worth comparing with the glory
that is going to be revealed to us."*
Romans 8:18 NKJV

~ Questions to Consider ~

Are you the one for whom God especially intended yesterday and today's verse?

~ Room for Reflection ~

Since God intended to use today's verse twice, what do you think He wants you to learn from it?

~ *Day 41* ~
On the Potter's Wheel

"He says, 'Be still, and know that I am God;'"
Psalm 46:10a NIV

~

"Sit still!" Did you ever have someone say those words to you, maybe as a child? Have you ever said it to one of your own children? Why is it sometimes necessary to be still? Imagine that you are a lump of clay, and a potter is ready to make you into a pitcher for holding water. If you were to squirm while on the potter's wheel, can you imagine what you might look like when he's finished? Not only would you look ridiculous, you might also not sit flat, or have a proper spout – you might not be fit for use.

God uses the analogy of Him as a potter and us as His clay many times throughout both the Old and New Testaments. He wants to remind us that He has a plan for our lives. But it requires our cooperation. When He says, "Go," we need to go. But when He says, "Be still," it's likely that He has some work to do that requires us to be still enough to hear His voice and for Him to work on smoothing out those rough edges. It means surrender. But the end result is always beautiful – a vessel fit for the Master's use.

~

Sit quietly upon the Potter's wheel;
And yield beneath His loving, skillful hand,
As tenderly He forms, within His plan,
The vessel he is longing to reveal.

Sit quietly, and feel Him work within.
Allow the firmness of His hand to smooth
Those stubborn flaws, till they have been removed;
And you've become a vessel fit for Him.

Sit quietly, and see what God will do;
As in His wisdom He reshapes, restores.
And through the transformation, joy is yours;
For He has set His heart on loving you.

~

Blessings in the Rain

"Yet you, LORD, are our Father.
We are the clay, you are the potter;
we are all the work of your hand."
Isaiah 64:8 NIV

~ Questions to Consider ~

Which is harder for you – going when God says, "Go"? Or being still when you'd rather be doing something else… anything other than that?

When is it easier to hear someone speaking to you – when you're still? Or when you're on the move?

If you're familiar with pottery, what goes into the process of molding a new project? How do rough edges become smooth? How is the pottery hardened?

How might that process apply to us as the clay?

~ Room for Reflection ~

What season does God have you in right now? A season of stillness? Or does He have you actively serving in a busier capacity?

If it's stillness, how are you doing? Are you thriving or struggling with the process? And how does trust fit in?

~ *Day 42* ~
A Hand to Hold through the Storm

Although it's usually what we pray for, God doesn't promise to take away our storms. But He does promise to walk with us THROUGH them.

~

Last night the wind was howling,
Which meant my dog was too.
And I knew from experience
Just what I had to do.

I gathered up my pillows,
Then headed down the stairs.
And when I reached the last step,
My trembling dog was there.

I lay down on the couch and
She lay down close beside.
And with my hand upon her,
I felt her fear subside.

I hadn't stopped the wind storm.
But she knew I was near.
And that was all she needed
To quickly calm her fear.

Sometimes our storms are like that –
God doesn't take away
The trial we are going through,
Though that is what we pray.

Instead, He moves in closer
And takes us by the hand,
So we will know He's with us and
It's all within His plan.

Blessings in the Rain

Then even though the winds howl,
We've strength to make it through;
For louder than the fiercest gale,
He whispers, "I'm here, too."

~

*"When you pass through the waters,
I will be with you;
and when you pass through the rivers,
they will not sweep over you.
When you walk through the fire,
you will not be burned;
the flames will not set you ablaze."
Isaiah 43:2 NIV*

~ Questions to Consider ~

*If you're currently going through a trial, or have recently faced one, did Jesus rescue you **from** it? Or walk with you **through** it?*

Are you familiar with the story of Shadrach Meshach and Abednego, from Daniel chapter 3? God didn't stop them from being thrown into the fiery furnace. But He went right in with them. Why do you suppose He sometimes chooses to let us walk through the trial?

~ Room for Reflection ~

If God asks you to walk through a trial rather than rescuing you from it, do you trust Him enough to believe it's for your good?

~ *Day 43* ~

Incubate My Faith

We want so desperately to fly. But nobody can fly right out of the shell.
It's time and testing that can give our faith wings to soar.

~

Lord, place me gently in Your faith-incubator;
for mine, within this fleshly shell,
is very small…weak and vulnerable.

Then bathe me
with the penetrating light of Your Spirit,
and the warmth of Your love.

Protect me
from the enemy's fiery darts
of doubt and discouragement,
that would pierce my fragile shell.

And as my faith begins to grow, Lord,
little by little, day by day,
send just enough nourishing trials
to help me grow,
without being overwhelmed
by more than I can bear.

And when my faith is ready, Lord ,
crack my shell.
so I can stretch and grow even more;
till my faith is ready to test its tiny wings,
on the wind of the very Spirit
that has warmed, nourished, and protected me…
the same Wind that now sustains me
as I wing my way through the calm and storms of life;
sometimes soaring, sometimes struggling;
but always upheld by You.

Blessings in the Rain

"The apostles said to the Lord,
"Increase our faith.""
Luke 17:5 ESV

~ Questions to Consider ~

What happens to a caterpillar if you free it from its cocoon, or a baby bird if its egg is cracked too soon?

Do you feel like your faith is already the strongest it could possibly be?

What could help strengthen your faith?

~ Room for Reflection ~

"Dear brothers and sisters, when troubles of any kind come your way, consider it an opportunity for great joy. For you know that when your faith is tested, your endurance has a chance to grow."
James 1:2-3 NLT

According to this verse, how do our faith and endurance grow?

~ Space for Grace ~

Take a few moments to thank God, today, for trials that have helped strengthen your faith.

~ Day 44 ~
Why, Lord?

" 'For my thoughts are not your thoughts,
neither are your ways my ways, '
declares the LORD."
Isaiah 55:8 NIV

~

Have you ever found yourself praying for healing, but no healing comes? And at the same time, someone else is also praying and is miraculously healed. Does that seem fair? Why would God heal one, and not another? Those times can be discouraging. Frustrating.

What encourages my heart is that God doesn't turn me away when I come to Him asking "why." He understands the cry of my heart. That doesn't mean He'll always give me the answer I'm looking for. Often His answer is Isaiah 55:8 (above). And that has to be enough.

My question for you, today, is this: do you trust that God's thoughts and ways are the very best for you? Do you trust HIM?

~

How is it, Lord, You sometimes choose
To spare a person's life;
But then You choose to take another's.
How can that be right?

For Lord, the way You pick and choose -
It doesn't quite seem fair,
Especially when they've both been covered
faithfully in prayer.

My child, I'm glad you've brought to Me
The questions on your heart.
I need for you to know you're seeing
Just a tiny part

Blessings in the Rain

Of what will be a masterpiece
In My sovereign design.
And one day you will see it too,
When it is fully time.

But until then, please trust Me, child;
For I can see what's best.
And I'll be working all things out
So My children are blessed.

~ Questions to Consider ~

Have you ever felt like God was unfair in the way He responds to your prayers? If so, what did you ask Him for?

If you've felt like your prayers went unanswered, why do you think God allowed the circumstances to continue that you asked Him to change?

~ Room for Reflection ~

Do you feel like you have freedom before God to ask Him "why?"

Do you feel like God loves you any less when He doesn't give you the answers you hoped for? Or do you trust Him enough to really believe His way and time are best?

~ *Day 45* ~
You've Never Been This Way

"Trust in the Lord with all your heart;
do not depend on your own understanding.
Seek his will in all you do,
and he will show you which path to take."
Proverbs 3:5-6 NLT

~

"Every day I traverse a new terrain, desperately dependent upon the
moment-by-moment guidance of Jesus because He is leading me into new
territory. He reminds me that my eyes must be fastened on Him, "then you
will know which way to go, since you have never been this way before"
(Joshua 3:4).[6] ~ Jennifer Kennedy Dean

~

My child,
you've never been
this way before
and do not know
the way

but I am
the Way-Maker
the Light-Giver
the Shepherd-Guide
to lead you
in the way
you should go

so stay close
follow Me
and I will
lead you home

~

Blessings in the Rain

"When you see the ark of the covenant of the LORD your God...
you are to move out from your positions and follow it.
Then you will know which way to go,
since you have never been this way before."
Joshua 3:3-4a NIV

~ Questions to Consider ~

Are you one to ask directions when you're lost?

How do you prepare ahead of time so it's less likely you'll end up on the wrong path?

Have you ever wished you had an ark, or cloud, or pillar of fire to lead the way like the Israelites did?

What do you have, today, to lead you in the right direction?

~ Room for Reflection ~

When you're setting out in a new direction, do you seek God and His direction first? Or do you tend to trust your own instincts and try to blaze your own trail?

And if you try it on your own first, do you find yourself frustrated, and having to go back to God to fix things, and lead you back to the path He had for you?

~ *Day 46* ~
Meant For Good

Are you familiar with the story of Joseph in the Old Testament - the guy with the coat of many colors? He was his father's favorite, among 12 sons; and his brothers hated him for it. They hated him so much they seriously considered murdering him. But instead they sold him into slavery. As a slave, he was unjustly accused of assaulting his master's wife, and was thrown into prison. He was stuck there several years until the king of Egypt had a dream and needed an interpreter. It was then that Joseph realized that all he had gone through was part of God's amazing plan to save the whole region, including his own family, from a terrible famine that might have destroyed them all. (Genesis 37-50)

Joseph's brothers sold him away into slavery. And perhaps it was Satan who caused the famine, hoping to wipe out the Israelite people. BUT GOD! (don't you just love those words?!). Here's what Joseph had to say about His ultimate plan for Joseph… and for you and me.

~

"But as for you, you meant evil against me;
but God meant it for good…"
Genesis 50:20a NKJV

~

What Satan means for evil,
To discourage and destroy,
Our God can turn to blessing;
Changing sorrow into joy.

For though He may allow us to
Be pressed on every side,
He won't let Satan crush us,
When it's in Him we abide.

He'll take those very things that seem
To lead us to despair,
And use them as a catalyst
To draw us into prayer.

Blessings in the Rain

And when He's gained the victory
By His own, mighty hand,
We'll find it is on solid ground
That, next to Him, we stand

To testify of His great love,
And His sustaining grace
That leads us from a precipice
Into a sheltered place;

Where, with thanksgiving, we can then
Endure, as Christians should.
For all that God allows in us,
He uses for our good.

~

"We are hard pressed on every side, but not crushed;
perplexed, but not in despair; All this is for your benefit,
so that the grace that is reaching more and more people
may cause thanksgiving to overflow to the glory of God."
2 Corinthians 4:8, 15 NIV

~ Room for Reflection ~

Have you ever experienced God turning what seemed a terrible
circumstance into something good on your behalf?

Is it difficult to imagine how God could manage to turn your current
circumstances into a blessing... something you can truly be thankful for?

Are you willing and able to thank God, even if you can't imagine how He
will work it out for your good?

~ *Day 47* ~
When the Miracle is Grace

"The LORD answered Moses, 'Is the LORD's arm too short? Now you will see whether or not what I say will come true for you.'"
Numbers 11:23 NIV

~

Do you ever wonder why we don't see the flashy miracles from God that they did in Bible times? Maybe the miracles Jesus is doing today are just as big, and just as powerful… but aren't the miracles we were looking and hoping for. His arm isn't any shorter to reach us today…

~

It's easy to be thankful when
God answers right away,
And when he sends the miracles
We ask for when we pray.

But what about those times it seems
Our prayer's been lost in space?
Friend, will we still be thankful when
The miracle is grace?

When we use circumstances as
A measure of God's love,
We may be missing many blessings
Sent down from above.

For sometimes God will send sufficient
Grace to see us through.
And that, friend, is a miracle –
A gift from God's hand, too.

So next time we are desperate for
Some miracle to come,
We're looking for God's hand to move
To help us overcome,

Blessings in the Rain

Let's keep in mind God's hand may move
A different time or place,
So we can then be thankful when
The miracle is grace.

~

"I was given a thorn in my flesh...
Three times I pleaded with the Lord to take it away from me.
But he said to me, 'My grace is sufficient for you,
for my power is made perfect in weakness.'"
2 Corinthians 12:7-9a NIV

~ Questions to Consider ~

God says His grace is sufficient for us. What is grace?

Have you ever experienced God's grace giving you the needed strength to get through a difficult time?

What miracle are you asking God for today?

~ Room for Reflection ~

Do you think right now that you would you be able to find peace and contentment if God's response to you is the same as it was to Paul in 2 Corinthians 12? Do you truly believe His grace can be enough for you?

~ *Day 48* ~
When I'm Covered with His Hand

"He hideth my soul in the cleft of the rock
That shadows a dry, thirsty land;
He hideth my life in the depths of His love,
And covers me there with His hand,
And covers me there with His hand."[7]
~ Fanny J. Crosby

~

Are you afraid of the dark? Many of us are, especially as children. Darkness makes it hard to see where we're going. It's hard to see the faces of those we love. Hard to see the blessings all around us.

But sometimes darkness is a place of protection. There's an account in the Old Testament where darkness was a good thing because it meant the very presence of God was nearer to Moses than it had ever been. You can find the full story in Exodus 33.

And I can't tell you how many testimonies I've heard from those who've gone through the darkest valleys – that those were the times they have felt closest to God because those are the times when they truly felt covered by His hand, or hidden beneath the shelter of His wings.

~

Sometimes it seems the darkest when
God's presence passes near.
His hand is stretched to cover us
So we cannot see clear
To gaze upon Him face to face;
But only, there, to see
The place where He passed by us as
He moved through sovereignly.
Then looking back where He has been,
We may not see His face;
But we'll be blessed to catch a glimpse
Of His amazing grace.

~

Blessings in the Rain

*"So it shall be, while My glory passes by,
that I will put you in the cleft of the rock,
and will cover you with My hand while I pass by."
Exodus 33:22 NKJV*

~ Questions to Consider ~

How do you normally react to darkness?

Have you ever been through a dark time where it seemed like God was nowhere to be found, but when looking back you could see His hand throughout the trial?

~ Room for Reflection ~

*"He will cover you with his feathers;
you will take refuge under his wings.
His faithfulness will be a protective shield.
You will not fear the terror of the night,
the arrow that flies by day,"
Psalm 91:4-5 CSB*

Next time you find yourself in a dark place, consider the possibility that Jesus is right there with you, covering you with His very own hand, or holding you extra close beneath His wing.

~ *Day 49* ~
An Arm Around Your Shoulder

"Put my tears into Your bottle;
Are they not in Your book?"
Psalm 56:8 NKJV

~

"In ancient egypt and palestine, women had the habit of collecting their tears shed during the mourning of a loved one and storing them in tear bottles. these bottles would be placed in the coffin or tomb with the deceased as a sign of their devotion."[8] Psalm 56 talks about God having a tear bottle, too. Isn't it amazing that the God of the universe not only knows and sees what we're going through, but even more importantly… He cares!

~

He wraps an arm around your shoulder, for He knows.
He seals each tear within His bottle, for He sees.
And when the pain goes deeper than the spoken word can say,
His own heart breaks to hear your silent pleas.

He's right beside you each and every moment that you hurt.
He's covering you now with angels' wings.
So lean into His bosom, as He longs to comfort you;
Just listen for the lullaby He sings.

For He is there, to wrap His arms around you,
To brush away each tear with His own hand.
And one day, up in glory, you will know the final joy
Of seeing how it all fit in His plan.

But for this day, just know He cares for you.
And even in this, He will see you through.

"casting all your care upon Him,
for He cares for you."
1 Peter 5:7 NKJV

~ Room for Reflection ~

If the Psalmist believes that God has a bottle for our tears, what does that tell you about God?

Do you believe He knows everything that's going on in your life?

Do you think He cares? What makes you think that?

Have you ever felt like you could almost literally feel Jesus wrap His arms around you? If so, what were the circumstances?

~ Space for Grace ~

If God has wrapped His arm around you in a difficult time, consider praying through these verses with gratitude: "All praise to God, the Father of our Lord Jesus Christ. God is our merciful Father and the source of all comfort. He comforts us in all our troubles so that we can comfort others. When they are troubled, we will be able to give them the same comfort God has given us." 2 Corinthians 1:3-4 NLT

~ *Day 50* ~
He's Everything to Me

I never labored over another poem like I did this one. It was a labor of love that took many months, and much Bible reading. Each description of God is taken from Scripture; and if you'd like a list of the Scripture references, you can contact me through the information at the back of this book, and I would be happy to share that list of verses with you.

My prayer is that these wouldn't be mere words on a page. But that through them I, and all those reading here, will come to know our God better: to know His character, and learn to recognize His voice. And find that He is, indeed, everything!

Almighty God – Jehovah – Savior - Pure and spotless Lamb
Creator of the universe -The only, great I AM
The Alpha and Omega - The Beginning and the End
The Bread of Life - The Vine - The Door - My Master – Teacher - Friend

The Loader-up of benefits - And Giver of good things
Oil Pourer - Joy Restorer - Glorious King of kings
Abba Father – Advocate - Sustainer of the weak
Chain Breaker - Peace Maker - Blesser of the meek

Star Namer - Lion Tamer - Singer over me
Dream Weaver - Fountain Cleaver - God who hears and sees
Defender and Deliverer - The Way - The Truth - The Life
The Bridegroom - The Anointed One - The Rock - The Word - The Light

Mountain Framer - Sea Restrainer - Rider on the wind
Giant Slayer - Ransom Payer - Pardoner of sin
Burden Bearer - Yoke Sharer - Tender to my cry
Throne Preparer - Breach Repairer - Dayspring from on High

Healer of the broken hearted - Opener of wombs
Promise Maker - Vengeance Taker - Vanquisher of tombs

Blessings in the Rain

Comforter – Redeemer – Helper - And my Hiding Place
Sea Divider - Need Provider - Lavisher of grace

Fashioner of beauty out of ashes that remained
Lion out of Judah that will not be cowed or tamed
Mountain Shaker - Seal breaker - Calmer of the waves
Veil Render - Lightning Sender - Lengthener of days

Setter up of kings and kingdoms - Raiser of dry bones
Drier-up of river beds - And precious Cornerstone
A Father to the fatherless - My Refuge – Strength - And Shield
My very present Help in trouble - By His stripes I'm healed

He's my Companion through the fire - Shelter in the flood
My God-in-flesh with Servant heart - And holy, righteous Judge
The Sun of Righteousness who comes with healing in His wings
And in the desert makes a way for clear, refreshing springs

My Intercessor - Counselor - The Writer of my name
The God who was, and is, and will forever be the same
The Lord of lords - The Prince of Peace - My all-Sufficiency
My Guide - My Portion - And my Hope –
He's everything to me!

~

*"Then Moses asked God, 'If I go to the Israelites and say to them:
The God of your fathers has sent me to you, and they ask me,
'What is His name?' what should I tell them?'
God replied to Moses, 'I AM WHO I AM.'"*
Exodus 3:13-14a HCSB

~ Room for Reflection ~

Now it's your turn! Do you know God personally? Who is He to you?

~ *Day 51* ~
Peace that Ransoms a Broken Heart

"just as the Son of Man did not come to be served, but to serve,
*and to give His life a **ransom** for many."*
Matthew 20:28 NIV

~

In February of 2016, a friend of mine put out a plea, asking for prayer for a friend who experienced some complications during childbirth. Her beautiful baby boy was born without a pulse, but otherwise perfectly healthy. We prayed and prayed that he would live. But after several days, the devastating news came that he had passed away. In the midst of profound sadness, however, they found purpose and joy as they were able to donate his organs to save the lives of several other babies.

They appropriately named him Ransom, which is a price paid to free someone else. Just as Jesus gave His life to ransom us, Ransom also gave his for others. It was some consolation to his family. But a deep and painful sacrifice, nonetheless. I wrote this for his family; and hope it encourages you today, especially if you're in a season of asking God "why."

~

When we're left with only questions,
And the tear stains on our cheeks,
When we've asked the Lord for mercy,
But His answer's left us weak

With our faith stretched past its limits,
And our hearts pierced through and through,
That is when we find in Jesus
That His heart is breaking, too.

For He hears our cries of anguish.
And He feels our deepest pain.
He is weeping there beside us
As He wipes each salty stain.

Blessings in the Rain

We are not alone in sorrow;
Jesus holds us in our grief.
As He wraps His arms around us,
We're surrounded by His peace.

Then He whispers that He loves us,
That He always has, and will;
That our prayers are not forgotten,
That He cares and loves us still.

And it's then our hearts surrender
Leaning hard into His breast,
Learning just how much He loves us;
Finding that His way is best.

~

*"Then you will experience God's peace,
which exceeds anything we can understand.
His peace will guard your hearts and minds
as you live in Christ Jesus."
Philippians 4:7 NLT*

~ Room for Reflection ~

Have you ever been in the midst of a trial, but rather than devastation, you experienced that supernatural peace that only God can give? What were those circumstances?

What does it mean to have peace guard your heart? What might God be guarding our hearts against?

~ *Day 52* ~
In the Eye of Your Storm

"And [Jesus] arose and rebuked the wind,
and said unto the sea, 'Peace, be still.'
And the wind ceased, and there was a great calm."
Mark 4:39 NKJV

~

I've never been in a hurricane. But I've seen videos from those who have, and it verifies what I learned in middle school science class – hurricanes have eyes. Not eyes that can see, of course. But with it's spiral shape, there is an area at its center around which the storm winds swirl. And in that center, there are no clouds; you can see straight up into the clear, blue sky, and the winds are calm.

Unfortunately for those going through a hurricane, the calm doesn't last. The back side of the storm soon moves in and the destructive winds and rain resume. And sometimes that's how life comes at us - one stormy gale after another. If that's where you are, look for Jesus. He's right there, offering you His peace in the midst of your storm.

~

Though a storm is raging all around you,
And though you've been beset by doubts and cares,
There is a place of peace amid the fury.
Child, look for Me, for I'll be there.

I'll meet you in the center of your storm;
And there you'll find a respite for your soul
As I remind you I am there with you,
And have the storm within my full control.

So when you are afraid, remember this -
That when it's time, I'll call out, "Peace, be still!"
And you will find your faith in Me grow stronger,
As you then see your storm bend to My will.

Blessings in the Rain

"Whenever I am afraid, I will trust in You."
Psalm 56:3 NKJV

~ Questions to Consider ~

What do you fear most? Physical pain? Emotional stress? Family trials?
What robs you of your peace?

How or where can you find peace in the middle of the storms in your life?

~ Room for Reflection ~

What does God want you to know about His love for you? How is it
demonstrated during our trials?

~ Space for Grace ~

~ Day 53 ~
Rest Now

Technology offers us the ability to do so much more than we ever could before. But there is something it doesn't offer that we all so desperately need...

~

"Come to Me, all of you who are weary and burdened,
and I will give you rest."
~ Jesus Christ (Matthew 11:28 HCSB)

~

Child, lay your head here gently on My chest,
And let your mind be perfectly at rest.
Don't let it fill with things you need to do.
But let this moment be just Me and you.

Those things you think cannot wait...well, they can.
Instead of yours, this time, let's try My plan.
For I see what tomorrow has in store.
It's all that you can bear, and nothing more.

There will be tests to stretch your growing faith.
There may be times to hurry...times to wait.
There may be times you feel you can't go on.
But in your weakness, child, I am strong.

I'm here with you today...tomorrow, too.
So rest, My child. And let Me care for you.

~

"casting all your care on Him,
because He cares about you."
1 Peter 5:7 HCSB

~ Questions to Consider ~

Do you believe that rest is important?

Do you believe that Jesus thinks rest is important? How do you know?

Do you get enough rest?

If yes, what do you do to be sure you get your rest? Does God play a part in your time of rest?

If you don't get enough rest, why not?

How does 1 Peter 5:7 impact your ability to find true rest and peace?

~ Room for Reflection ~

What does true rest feel like?

What changes might you need to make in order to get needed rest?

~ *Day 54* ~
sweetness reigns

Cancer. There it was... again. THAT word.

She had been down that road before. We had prayed. Remission. But back it came, and with a vengeance. Through it all, Rosemary never lost her faith, or her joy. She continued to look for the blessings in every day, right up until her graduation to Glory.

Rosemary shared these words on Facebook, in the midst of some of her darkest days. I wrote back with the words that follow, inspired by her steadfast faith. If you are in a season of grey days, perhaps they will bring you some measure of encouragement, too.

~

"Grey days are not welcome.
But sweetness reigns...
and all is right with the world."
~ Rosemary Marino, Facebook post 7/27/12

~

sweetness reigns –
in scents and sounds
of summer rain.
for though the day is grey,
the grass will be greener
and the flowers far lovelier
when the showers have passed.

sweetness reigns –
even in the midst
of suffering and pain.
for Grace is far nearer.
and those who love us best
show it most
when we are most in need.

Blessings in the Rain

yes, sweetness reigns…
and all is right with the world
when my world is right with the Lord,
and His sweetness reigns.

~

"…in the clefts of the rock,
in the crevices of the cliff,
let me see your face, let me hear your voice;
for your voice is sweet, and your face is lovely."
Song of Solomon 2:14 HCSB

~ Space for Grace ~

Taking my cue from Rosemary, I'm going to leave the remaining space on this day for the sweet things, the blessings in your life today. Look around you. Outside of your trial, or maybe even within it. What do you see? Can you find the grace?

~ *Day 55* ~
Worth the Wait

"But if we hope for what we do not yet have,
we wait for it patiently."
Romans 8:25 NIV

~

There's that word again – Wait. And to make it worse, we're supposed to do it patiently? Seems like that's asking a lot! I don't know about you, but if I can see God at work, I can be patient. Or if I'm certain of the outcome, I don't mind the wait quite as much. But oftentimes God asks us to wait patiently when we see no signs of activity from Him, and have no clue of the outcome.

And yet God says, "Be patient. Wait. Trust Me!"

~

What is it with this waiting, God?
We've got big things to do!
Perhaps I'll get to work, and then
Come check back in with You.

At least then I'd being doing something,
Not sitting around.
That surely won't accomplish much.
Feels like we're losing ground…

But what's your hurry, child? Can you
See past this point in time?
Whose plan do you think might be best?
Your hasty one… or Mine?

Remember in the waiting there
Is time for you to grow.
And though you cannot see it there
Are things you still don't know.

Blessings in the Rain

So trust Me, child. Slow down, and wait.
My timing will be best.
And I will be at work so you,
In waiting, will be blessed.
~

"Wait for the Lord;
be strong and take heart
and wait for the Lord."
Psalm 27:14 NIV

~ Questions to Consider ~

Is there some unanswered prayer testing your patience right now? If so, what are you waiting for?

Are you confident enough in God's wisdom and timing to wait patiently for Him to answer your prayer?

~ Room for Reflection ~

Why do you think God is delaying answering your prayers? What might He be wanting to teach you as you wait?

Are you teachable as you wait? Or stubborn?

~ *Day 56* ~
Secure In God's Hands

"I have held many things in my hands,
and I have lost them all;
but whatever I have placed in God's hands,
that I still possess."
~ Martin Luther

~

Those things that I clench tightly in my hands
Slip through my fingers, just like shifting sands.
But those entrusted to my Father's care
I know, deep in my heart, will still be there
Until the end of time, and then beyond.
For He's the one I can depend upon
To hold together all of time and space;
And yet, in His amazing, matchless grace
Still hold even my smallest hopes and dreams;
Because He loves and cares for even me.

~

"But whatever were gains to me
I now consider loss for the sake of Christ.
What is more, I consider everything a loss
because of the surpassing worth
of knowing Christ Jesus my Lord..."
Philippians 3:7-8 NIV

~

~ Room for Reflection ~

What would be the most difficult things for you to give back to God, if He asked you to do so?

Would you be willing to do so? Why or why not?

~ Space for Grace ~

Consider writing a prayer –
of gratitude for all that God has given you,
of confession for holding onto some of those things too tightly,
and of willingness to give back to Him whatever or whoever He might ask.

~ *Day 57* ~
Lord, Rain on Us!

This book was written for and dedicated to my friend Donna Bartz, who is currently battling lung cancer. She has claimed *#BlessingsInTheRain* as her focus through this journey. And these are her own words –

"I felt like every day something was being taken from me," Donna said. *"But when (the Lord) looks down on me I want Him to say there's all this evil and terrible things in this world, but from this house I see peace and I see joy, and I see her, in spite of her suffering, reflecting my glory."[9]*

And these are the words of her husband John, following one of her many surgeries, *"Donna and I begin every day asking 'what blessings will we see today?' We can honestly say despite the storm we have seen many #BlessingsInTheRain."[10]*

~

Shower us, Lord, we pray
With Your blessings from above –
Your mercy and forgiveness,
Your wisdom, grace and love.

And Lord, when raindrops catch us
By undesired surprise,
Remind us that Your blessings
Come sometimes in disguise.

Then when those blessings tarry,
As they so often do,
Please hold our hands much tighter
As we yield, Lord, to You.

For oh, the sweet surrender
Of bowing to Your will,
Of waiting for those blessings
You've promised, Lord, until

Blessings in the Rain

Your clouds burst with abundance
Of soul-refreshing grace,
As we look up with wonder, Lord,
To find Your smiling face.

~

*For "God is able to bless you abundantly,
so that in all things at all times,
having all that you need,
you will abound in every good work."
2 Corinthians 9:8 NIV*

~ Room for Reflection ~

Are you in the midst of a trial that has you searching a little harder for those blessings in disguise?

~ Space for Grace ~

List some blessings you've been finding in this season of life, especially the ones that don't necessarily feel like blessings in the moment. How has God turned them into joy for you?

~ *Day 58* ~
Through Gates of Glory

Sometimes we pray, and God answers, "Yes!" But sometimes He says, "I have a better plan," and that plan is hard to bear. Will we keep trusting that He desperately loves us and is working all things out for our good, even then?

~

" 'My thoughts are nothing
like your thoughts,' says the Lord.
'And my ways are far beyond
anything you could imagine.'"
Isaiah 55:8 NLT

~

When healing doesn't come this side of Heaven,
It doesn't mean God loves us any less;
Or that our prayers were lacking, faith was weak...
It means He chose a different way to bless.

It may not be what we had hoped or prayed for.
It may feel like He didn't care enough
To send the healing touch we all were wanting.
But oftentimes it's just not clear to us

How much He loves, and just what His love looks like.
We think that grace and healing are the same.
But God just doesn't think or work like we do.
His grace is on a higher, deeper plain.

So when the healing comes through gates of Glory,
There is no struggle lost. No prayer unmet.
Instead, it means God had a better answer
That we, through tear-stained eyes, can't see just yet.

Blessings in the Rain

But one day, up in Glory, we will understand
The wisdom and the love behind His will.
Until that day, friend, we can choose to trust Him,
And in the sad times, glorify Him, still.

~

*"And we know that all things work together for good to those who love
God, to those who are the called according to His purpose."*
Romans 8:28 NKJV

~ Questions to Consider ~

*Has God chosen to take someone you love Home to Heaven rather than
healing them here?*

*Is God asking you or someone you love to bear the cross of a terminal
disease?*

~ Room for Reflection ~

*Do you ever feel like maybe God loves someone else more than He loves
you because He gave them what they asked for?*

*How can you be convinced that God loves you very deeply, even when it
seems like He's not answering your prayers?*

What does Jeremiah 29:11 tell you about God's plans for you?

~ *Day 59* ~
Only a Breath of Praise Away

Are you waiting and praying for a miracle? Don't give up! Don't grow discouraged! Perhaps...

"our miracle is one more breath of praise away."
Nita Myers Gagliano, Facebook 4/21/13
~

I breathed a breath of praise today.
He heard,
for He's no more
than just a breath away.

And in that breath He heard
the trust,
the hope of things unseen
in just a single word...

Halleluiah.

Halleluiah, though the road is long.
And hard.
And I am
Anything but strong.

Halleluiah, though the pain is real.
And unrelenting.
And all that's left
Is faith that He can heal.

And there it is,
in the halleluiah...
The miracle of joy!
And peace. And grace.

Blessings in the Rain

The knowing that His way is always best.
And good.
And that His name is Love.
And I am blessed.

And never will I ever doubt again
the truth –
that miracles still happen…
and mine
is close at hand.
~
"Do not be anxious about anything,
but in every situation, by prayer and petition,
with thanksgiving, present your requests to God."
Philippians 4:6 NIV

~ Room for Reflection ~

Can you praise the name of Jesus today, despite your current circumstances?

What's holding back your Halleluiah's today?

~ Space for Grace ~

What can you find joy in today?

~ *Day 60* ~
Turner of Tides

Are you asking the Lord to turn things around for you? He can, you know…

~

"…but the Lord your God turned the curse into a blessing for you, because the Lord your God loves you."
Deuteronomy 23:5b NKJV

~

He turns my curse to blessing,
And sorrow into joy.
He takes my fear and gives me peace
That nothing can destroy.

He gives beauty for ashes,
And sweet freedom for chains.
He comforts me through mourning and
Gives cause for sweet refrains.

And all because He loves me
Much more than I could know.
I search my Bible daily for
It's there He tells me so.

That's why even in hard times
I can be satisfied,
'Cause Jesus is my Savior and
The Turner of the Tide.

~

Blessings in the Rain

"...the Lord has anointed Me
To preach good tidings to the poor;
He has sent Me to heal the brokenhearted,
To proclaim liberty to the captives,
And the opening of the prison to those who are bound...
To console those who mourn in Zion,
To give them beauty for ashes,
The oil of joy for mourning,
The garment of praise for the spirit of heaviness;"
Isaiah 61:1-3a NKJV

~ Questions to Consider ~

Has it been feeling like the tide is pushing or pulling you in the wrong direction?

Do you need to know today that God can turn your ashes into something beautiful?

~ Room for Reflection ~

"For with God nothing will be impossible." Luke 1:37 NKJV

What might this verse mean for you, today?

~ *Day 61* ~
Still There

Sometimes we pray, asking God to move in our lives, and all we hear back is crickets. Silence. Almost as if our prayers didn't make it past the ceiling. Or maybe God was too busy helping everyone else and didn't have time for us.

Could you use a little reminder today that God is still there, actively moving in your life... even if you can't see or feel Him? He is! and wants to calm all your fears and anxiety because He so deeply loves you!

~

"But the LORD is still there."
Zephaniah 3:5 NLT

~

Darkness may be settling in –
But the LORD is still there!

Walls may feel like they're closing in –
But the LORD is still there!

Fear and doubt may raise their hopeless heads –
But the LORD is still there!

Loneliness may ache like a heart too bruised to beat –
But the LORD is still there!

and *"With His love, He will calm all your fears."*
Zephaniah 3:17 NLT

~

~ Questions to Consider ~

Have you ever been through a time when it was hard to sense God's presence or love in your life? If so, what was happening at that time?

What, if anything, helped change that perception?

~ Room for Reflection ~

It's one thing to know, in your head, that God is with you. But sometimes quite another to really KNOW it, to feel it in your bones, and sense it undeniably in your heart. What can you do in those times when you don't FEEL it, to help yourself truly know that He really is there? Maybe start with this prayer-verse:

"I do believe, but help me overcome my unbelief!"
Mark 9:24 NLT

~ *Day 62* ~
Waiting in the Wings

*"but they who **wait** for the L*ORD
shall renew their strength;
they shall mount up with wings like eagles;
they shall run and not be weary;
they shall walk and not faint."
Isaiah 40:31 ESV

~

Wait... it's such a hard word. Such a stressful place to be. But when the waiting room is beneath the wings of an all-knowing, all-powerful God, it can be just a little bit easier. Stretchful rather than stressful.

~

When answers are not coming as
I seek God's face in prayer,
When I have watched and listened but
I just can't feel Him there,

When things seem to be getting worse,
And it's hard to believe,
That's not the time to turn away
For God's still holding me.

His answers may seem slow in coming;
But they're not, to Him.
He knows just when it's best, and He'll
Not answer until then.

He's teaching me to trust more through
The deepest, hardest things.
And all the while, I'm tucked in safely –
Waiting in His wings.

~

Blessings in the Rain

"...in the shadow of your wings I will take refuge,
till the storms of destruction pass by.
I cry out to God Most High,
to God who fulfills his purpose for me.
He will send from heaven and save me...
God will send out his
steadfast love and his faithfulness!"
Psalm 57:1-3 ESV

~ Questions to Consider ~

Are you currently in one of life's waiting rooms? In a providential holding
pattern? If so, what are you waiting for?

What words come to mind when you think of a chick under its mother's
wing?

~ Room for Reflection ~

Do any of those words you wrote down describe how you're feeling right
now? If yes, thank God for placing you in His wonderful care. If no,
perhaps you could ask Him to help you nestle into that space where He
can best shelter and care for you.

~ *Day 63* ~

A Pilgrim's Song

Sometimes I have this feeling that I just don't belong here. That maybe I was made for a different place and time? There's a good reason we feel that way, you know. Those of us who have given our lives to Jesus are simply traveling through, on our way to something else, some place far better. We don't fit in here because we're made for Heaven.

~

"...they were longing for a better country—a heavenly one.
Therefore God is not ashamed to be called their God,
for he has prepared a city for them."
Hebrews 11:16 NIV

~

I'm just a weary pilgrim,
And only passing through
On my way to a city
That's just beyond my view.

And I've a certain promise –
A home waits there for me
Where I will be with Jesus
For all eternity.

So I'll be moving on now.
I'm not content to stay
When I hear Jesus calling,
And leading me away.

Oh, won't you join me, pilgrim?
The path is just ahead.
It isn't wide or easy;
But there, I'm Spirit-fed.

Blessings in the Rain

And blessings fall like raindrops,
To cool me on the way
As I just follow Jesus,
And He leads, day by day.

Then when I see that city,
I'll finally be at home;
With no more storms or trials,
And no more need to roam.

Just God, my Heavenly Father,
And all the saints I've loved;
At home with Christ, my Savior,
In Heaven, up above.

"What a day that will be!"
~

*"By faith [Abraham] made his home in the promised land
like a stranger in a foreign country...For he was looking forward to the
city with foundations, whose architect and builder is God."
Hebrews 11:9-10 NIV*

~ Room for Reflection ~

Do you ever have that same feeling? Like you just don't fit in here?

*Where or when do you feel most at home? Is it with other Christians? Do
brothers and sisters in Christ feel like family, and more like home?*

~ *Day 64* ~

A Prayer of Surrender and a Sigh of Relief

I have to admit that there are times, probably many times, that I've taken a burden to the Lord, surrendered it to Him… then picked it right back up to carry it some more myself; or offered God advice on how it should best be handled. I suppose that means I don't truly trust God to carry it better for me. So I invite you to NOT be like me. Cast those cares on Him, trust Him, and leave them there!

~

It's not my job to help God out
And formulate a plan.
Instead I am to trust Him as
I take hold of His hand,

And follow where He leads me,
Taking one step at a time;
Carefully treading in His footprints,
Not retracing mine.

For He already knows the plan
He's got in mind for me.
And it is both for my own good,
And His ultimate glory.

He's proven time and time again
To be faithful and true.
So laying down my plan for His
Is what I've got to do.

And it's a happy yielding, for
No longer do I bear
The burden of my future plans.
I've yielded them in prayer.

Blessings in the Rain

And I'll rest, knowing things are best
Left to His sovereign plans.
Cuz there's no better place than in
The hollow of His hands.

~

" 'For I know the plans I have for you,' declares the Lord,
'plans to prosper you and not to harm you,
plans to give you hope and a future.'"
Jeremiah 29:11 NIV

~ Questions to Consider ~

Are you good at surrendering your burdens to the Lord? Or are you more like me, taking them back on your own shoulders?

~ Room for Reflection ~

Why do we tend to pick our burdens back up, rather than leaving them at the throne of Jesus?

What are you holding onto that God is inviting you to surrender to Him?

What's going on in your life right now for which you need to know God has a good plan?

~ *Day 65* ~
With a Heavy Heart

We sat in stunned silence as she shared about the tragic accident, and how her sweet friend would not be coming home from work that day. She left behind a husband who adored her, and two little girls whose lives would never be the same.

What does one say in a moment like that? We search for words. But sometimes there just aren't any. And in those moments, the Holy Spirit moves in close and whispers, "I'm here. And I've got this."

~

"But the Holy Spirit prays for us with groanings
that cannot be expressed in words.
And the Father who knows all hearts
knows what the Spirit is saying,
for the Spirit pleads for us believers
in harmony with God's own will."
Romans 8:26b-27 NIV

~

It's when my heart's too heavy even for a prayer
That Jesus whispers tenderly that He is there,
And that His shoulder's broad enough to lean upon
As He waits with me quietly till comes the dawn.

But dawn is slow in coming, as the tears still flow.
Yet He is there beside me; and I come to know
How deep His love, how gentle His amazing grace;
And how secure I am when in His warm embrace.

And even in my deepest pain, I find His peace.
It floods my soul and gives my sorrow sweet release.
Then as I lay it all on Him, He bids me rise.
He lifts my chin so I can look into His eyes;

Blessings in the Rain

And there I find a love that will not let me go,
Assurance far beyond the faith I used to know,
A comfort deep within I had not found before,
And grace to heal the pain, to strengthen and restore.

For when my heart is heavy, Jesus meets me there;
And He's a friend who's closer even than a prayer.

~

"Praise be to the God and Father of our Lord Jesus Christ,
the Father of compassion and the God of all comfort,
who comforts us in all our troubles…"
2 Corinthians 1:3-4a NIV

~ Room for Reflection ~

It is in those moments when God is all we have, that we learn He is all we need. He knows exactly how to comfort us, and give us His peace that surpasses any human understanding.

Have you been in a position where a friend needed comfort, but you didn't know what to say or do to really help?

Have you been in the other position, desperately needing comfort and peace, but unable to find it in family or friends?

Were you able to find the peace of God in the midst of your pain? If so, how did He reveal Himself? How did He help you?

~ *Day 66* ~
He Is Our Peace

Peace. Lasting Peace. Do you have it? Do you know where to find it? Not in a place. Not in a thing. But a WHO.

~

"For he himself is our peace…"
Ephesians 2:14a NIV

~

He is our peace when all around the storm is raging.
He is our peace when no one seems to care.
And when we find no comfort in the words of those around us,
The peace we find in Christ is always there.

He is our peace when those we love are taken.
He is our peace, even amidst our pain.
And when the enemy would whisper words of deep despair,
The peace of Christ sweeps through us, once again.

He is our peace when we face persecution.
He is our peace through all our suffering.
And when we fear we've reached the end of all that we can bear,
His peace will still allow our hearts to sing.

Oh, what a wondrous peace we have in Jesus.
Just knowing that He was and is the same
Assures us that His peace won't fade with time or circumstance;
For its foundation is His precious Name.

~

Blessings in the Rain

[Jesus said] "I am leaving you with a gift—
peace of mind and heart.
And the peace I give is a gift
the world cannot give.
So don't be troubled or afraid."
John 14:27 NLT

~ Questions to Consider ~

What does peace feel like? What other words can you use to describe how it feels in your own life?

Is it possible to have peace when a storm is raging all around you?

Do you have peace? If so, where and how did you find it?

~ Room for Reflection ~

One of the greatest things this world is missing and can't seem to find is lasting peace? What can you do to help others find that kind of peace?

~ *Day 67* ~
Believing Even When I Don't Feel It

"Now faith is confidence in what we hope for
and assurance about what we do not see."
Hebrews 11:1 NIV

~

Have you ever noticed how easily a flag moves in just the slightest breeze.
The same is true for leaves on most trees. If we try to determine if the
wind is blowing by looking for swaying trees or blowing sand, we might
be fooled into thinking the wind isn't blowing at all. But sometimes it
blows so gently that it's almost unnoticeable. Whether or not we can feel it
ourselves doesn't determine it's motion; only our perception of it.

And the same can be said for God's own Holy Spirit...

I noticed as I walked this morning
I could feel no breeze,
Nor was there any stirring in
The now leaf-barren trees.

But then my eyes were drawn to something
Swirling in the air.
A flag was waving gently for
Indeed the wind was there.

God's Spirit moves like that, at times;
I may not feel His touch.
But He is moving, just the same;
His hand perfecting much.

And that is where my faith comes in –
When I'm confident of
A God whose face I cannot see,
But know His name is Love.

Blessings in the Rain

For moments when I do not feel
That measure of His grace,
I only need to look around
For glimpses of His face.

And He is ever faithful, proving
Time and time again
That He is there to lend His grace;
My sure and faithful Friend.

~

"May your gracious Spirit lead me forward..."
Psalm 143:10a NLT

~ Questions to Consider ~

How do you know the Holy Spirit is with you? What does He do in your life?

~ Room for Reflection ~

Do you remember what life was like before the Holy Spirit was with you? How have things changed?

~ Space for Grace ~

Take some time to thank God for the gift of the Holy Spirit, and how He moves in your heart and life.

~ *Day 68* ~
Opener of Windows

My friend Cindy has faced many struggles in her life, but always does so with great grace and unwavering faith. Not long ago, she shared this secret with the world. And it makes all the difference!

~

"My heart is sinking, I'm so afraid...
I see no way out, no escape.
But my faith reminds me that You are
the Creator of doors and open windows."
~ *Cindy Tamboso*

~

When my heart is sinking
And I feel afraid,
I turn to my Father,
Bow my head, and pray:

Opener of windows,
Creator of new doors,
Revealer of the pathway
That wasn't there before;

Parter of the waters,
Splitter of the stone;
I will trust none other
Than You, oh Lord, alone.

Though my heart is fearful,
Still I'll trust in You;
For You have been faithful
In everything You do.

Blessings in the Rain

So Lord, I'll be waiting;
I'll be still, and see
How You will deliver
And work Your best, for me.

~

"I will love You, O LORD, my strength.
The LORD is my rock and
my fortress and my deliverer;
My God, my strength, in whom I will trust;"
Psalm 18:1-2a NKJV

~ Questions to Consider ~

Has God ever opened a new door for you? If so, what did that new door lead to?

~ Room for Reflection ~

Do you believe that the God who did amazing miracles – parting the sea, splitting open a rock for water, opening jail cells – do you believe THAT God is still the same God today? If so, what could He do for you?

When God opens new doors or windows, are you quick to walk through them? Or do you tend to hold back until you feel like you have all the details you deem necessary?

~ *Day 69* ~
Nothing Wasted

I love doing jigsaw puzzles. The harder, the better! But I recently faced my worst puzzle-nightmare: I got to the end of the puzzle, and the last piece was missing. UGH! It's the worst!!! I looked for days, not willing to take it apart until it was complete. Then the day I finally resolved to put it away, finished or not, I found the missing piece hiding under the leg of our coat rack. Oh, happy day!

I'm so thankful that Jesus never loses pieces of our puzzles. He never gets to the end to find pieces that didn't fit. He never gets frustrated to the point of giving up. And it all goes together, in His hands, to form a perfect picture.

~

When God is at work
in me
and in you
nothing is wasted

There are no
extra pieces
that don't fit
somewhere
in the puzzle

there are no
broken pieces
that He cannot
gather up
and put back together

Blessings in the Rain

He is
the Puzzle Solver
the Piece Gatherer
the Joy Restorer
who works
ALL things
together
for good
so nothing is wasted
~

"[Jesus]said to his disciples,
'Gather the pieces that are left over.
Let nothing be wasted.'"
John 6:12b NIV

~ Questions to Consider ~

Do you ever feel like there are pieces of your life that just don't fit? What
part of your current life just doesn't make sense right now?

~ Room for Reflection ~

Have you ever tried to put a puzzle together without a picture of how it
should look when it's finished? God sees our finished picture. We don't.
Who do you think would do a better job putting the pieces together?

~ Space for Grace ~

Take a moment to be thankful that Jesus never loses pieces, puts them in
the wrong place, or finds a broken one He can't fix.

~ *Day 70* ~
When God Could Have, But Didn't

for those times when God, in His great wisdom and love, says "No."

~

"As the heavens are higher than the earth,
so are my ways higher than your ways
and my thoughts than your thoughts."
Isaiah 55:9 NIV

~

When God could have but He didn't,
Will my faith still be as strong?
Or will I lower expectations,
Wondering what went wrong?

If God's arms had been longer
Could He then have saved the day?
If He had been more powerful
Could He have made a way?

If He'd just stepped in sooner would
There be no need to cry?
So here I am left wondering…
If God is Love, then why?

It's then I hear His Spirit in
His own, most tender way,
Speak right into my very heart
And oh so sweetly say,

"You are my precious child, and
I could not love you more.
And what you see as failure, child,
Will be another door;

Blessings in the Rain

A threshold you must walk through
To reach a brand new place
Of greater faith and courage,
A stronger sense of grace.

So child, if I didn't…
Please trust that it was best.
For I love you far more than
To give you something less."

~

*"Surely the arm of the Lord is not too short to save,
nor his ear too dull to hear."
Isaiah 59:1 NIV*

~ Room for Reflection ~

*Is it difficult to imagine that the most loving thing God could say to you is,
"No?"*

*If you have children of your own, do you ever tell them "no?" If you do,
why?*

*Have you ever considered that your Heavenly Father might have the same
reasons for saying "no" as we do with our children?*

~ Space for Grace ~

Can you thank God for the times when He has said "No" to you?

~ *Day 71* ~
Come, Find It in Me

Searching for peace? Here's a suggestion...

~

You've searched this world for peace –
In faces full of promise, till
The promise breaks and leave you still
In need of sweet release.

You've searched for peace again –
In arms outstretched to welcome you
Until they selfishly withdrew
As new trials began.

You've searched for peace and found
That it can be a fragile thing
In times of trial and suffering
When doubt and fear abound.

So find your peace in Me.
The peace I offer comes from hands
Pierced deep by love that understands
Exactly what you need.

And My hands won't let go.
They've overcome the world for you.
They purchased peace and pardon, too,
Because I love you so.

~

"I have told you these things, so that in me you may have peace.
In this world you will have trouble. But take heart!
I have overcome the world."
John 16:33 NIV

~ Room for Reflection ~

This isn't our first look at peace in this devotional book. What do you believe God is wanting you to learn about peace?

Do others see you as someone who has found peace?

What would you tell someone who asks you where you find peace?

~ Space for Grace ~

~ *Day 72* ~
When Things Seem to Get Worse Instead of Better

Have you ever prayed about something, or done something you knew God was asking of you, only to have things go from bad to worse? Sometimes that happens. Just ask Moses…

~

"Then Moses went back to the Lord and protested,
'Why have you brought all this trouble on your own people, Lord?
Why did you send me? Ever since I came to Pharaoh as your spokesman,
he has been even more brutal to your people.
And you have done nothing to rescue them!'"
Exodus 5:22-23 NLT

~

When things seem to be getting worse,
Please don't misunderstand.
It isn't that God's not at work,
Or has withdrawn His hand.

It's only when a puzzle's done,
The final piece in place,
That we can see the finished work –
God's wisdom, love and grace.

So when it seems God hasn't heard,
Or worse… He doesn't care,
That's not the time to give up hope.
Keep seeking Him in prayer.

He is at work on your behalf.
And one day you will see
Deliverance so amazing that
There's no doubt it must be

Blessings in the Rain

God working all things out for you,
In perfect harmony,
The pieces falling into place;
And to Him… all the glory!

~

*"Then the Lord told Moses, 'Now you will see what I will do…
I am the Lord. I will free you from your oppression…
I will redeem you with a powerful arm …
I will claim you as my own people, and I will be your God.
Then you will know that I am the Lord your God…'"*
Exodus 6:1,6-7 NLT

~ Questions to Consider ~

Have you ever prayed for someone, or something, only to see things get worse (or at least seem to)?

When that happens, do you assume you did something wrong? Heard God wrong? Didn't pray the right way?

~ Room for Reflection ~

What might be another reason for what happened when you prayed or followed God's leading?

~ *Day 73* ~
Daybreak

For those of you waiting for the dark of night to be lifted,
for a glimpse of sunlight…

~

"God shall help her, just at the break of dawn."
Psalm 46:5b NKJV

~

Pink is spreading through the sky.
The morning's finally come and I,
Through tears of joy, welcome the dawn.
For night has been both hard and long.

But with the rising of the sun
Comes joy in what my God has done,
As He walked with me through the black
Of darkest night, and drew me back

To greet the new day, in its grace,
With greater peace and growing faith
From all I learned that long, cold night –
To walk by faith, and not by sight.

Your Word says joy comes with the dawn.
Lord, here we are. You were not wrong;
For greater joy I've never known,
But found, at last, in You alone.

~

"Weeping may endure for a night,
But joy comes in the morning"
Psalm 30:5b NKJV

~ Questions to Consider ~

Where are you right now? Still groping through the dark of night? Seeing the first shades of dawn? Finally where you can see the sun shining again?

~ Room for Reflection ~

Have you ever been in a place so dark that it felt you might never see the light of day again... like things would never again be right?

If so, were you aware of the promises from Psalms that it wouldn't last forever? And did those promises help to encourage you at all?

What might you say to a friend who is going through a dark time in their life? (Sometimes there are no right words. Sometimes they're not yet ready to hear them. But it's great to be prepared for when those opportunities to encourage someone do come.)

~ *Day 74* ~
Outrageous Grace

Who wouldn't want that?!
~

"For from his fullness we have all received,
grace upon grace.*"*
John 1:16 ESV

~

outrageous grace
flung from the coffers of Heaven
upon the eager, upturned faces
of those who count it all joy
to dance before His throne

to dance
when the brilliant sunlight
bathes them
in its abundant
warmth and beauty

to dance still
in the gloomy shadow
of a gray and menacing cloud

to keep dancing
when the chilling rain
begins inevitably to fall

and to dance with abandon
when the prismic sunlight
bends those drenching rains
into promising rainbows

Blessings in the Rain

only grace
outrageous grace
God's grace
inspires such dancing
as this

~

"And God is able to bless you abundantly,
so that in all things at all times,
having all that you need,
you will abound in every good work."
2 Corinthians 9:8 NIV

~ Room for Reflection ~

Grace is God's undeserved kindness or favor. Sometimes it comes
wrapped in pretty bows and is just what we prayed for. But other times it
comes disguised as trials. I hope the words of this poem encourage you to
celebrate God's grace, regardless of the packaging.

What evidences of God's grace do you see in your life today?

How can 2 Corinthians 9:8 encourage you to be thankful, even for the
blessings in disguise?

~ *Day 75* ~
His Voice in the Storm

When storms come, there is nearly always someone whispering to us that all is lost. That we might just as well give up. That God must not truly love us. Friend, that is the voice of the thief, coming to rob you of your joy and peace. Pay no attention to that voice! Listen, instead, to the Shepherd who loves you, and who has promised to work it all out for your good.

~

"The thief's purpose is to steal and kill and destroy.
My purpose is to give them
a rich and satisfying life."
John 10:10 NLT

~

There is an enemy afoot.
He's out to steal your joy.
He aims to take your peace, as well.
The tactics he'll employ

Are fear and doubt…discouragement,
As swirling storms surround.
But friend, God's whisp'ring to your heart,
"You're still on solid ground.

It might not feel that way; you may
Feel hope is all but lost.
But fix your eyes on Me, not on
Those waves that turn and toss.

For I'm still in control, and this
Will end just when it should.
And what the devil means for harm –
I'll use it for your good.

Blessings in the Rain

So though the storm still rages, it
Will end just as I've planned.
And while you wait, I'll send that peace
You cannot understand.

For I'm still Abba Father you
Have come to trust and know.
And in the end, yes, even this
Will say, 'I love you so!'"
~
"Don't worry about anything;
instead, pray about everything.
Tell God what you need,
and thank him for all he has done.
Then you will experience God's peace,
which exceeds anything we can understand.
His peace will guard your hearts and minds
as you live in Christ Jesus."
Philippians 4:6-7 NLT

~ Questions to Consider ~

What's causing you to worry, doubt, or feel discouraged today?

What does God invite us to do with those feelings and concerns?

~ *Day 76* ~
Be Strong and Courageous

She came home from her doctor's appointment with stunning news. My friend had a very serious medical condition that required immediate surgery. Thing is, she had just lost her husband very unexpectedly, so she and their two young children were still reeling from the weariness, pain, and grief of their loss. How could she possibly find the strength for such a thing?

There's only one place to find strength like that, and the peace and courage necessary to do what was needed. She knew just where to go… into the arms of Jesus.

I wrote this for Beth, and gave it to her the night before her surgery. I hope it will be an encouraging reminder to you as well, that whatever battle you're facing, you're not in it alone.

~

Child, be strong and courageous;
I'm in this fight with you.
And I'll supply the strength you need,
And grace to see you through.

At times it's going to feel like
You can't take any more.
But keep in mind the times I've fought
Alongside you before.

And child, if you grow weary,
And lack the strength to stand,
I'll be right here to lean upon;
Just take hold of My hand.

Blessings in the Rain

And this, child, is My promise –
My mercies will be yours,
As you see how My faithful hand
Rebuilds, renews… restores.

~

"…Be strong and courageous.
Do not be afraid; do not be discouraged,
for the LORD your God will be with you
wherever you go."
Joshua 1:9 NIV

~ Questions to Consider ~

When has it been hardest in your life to find courage?

When have you seen God give you the greatest strength and peace?

When have you seen your faith grow the most?

~ Room for Reflection ~

Were all of the above answers the same?

~ *Day 77* ~
Take It to Jesus

"Cast all your anxiety on him
because he cares for you."
1 Peter 5:7 NIV

~

As I was reading that familiar verse, 1 Peter 5:7, it occurred to me how appropriate it was that a fisherman (Peter) would use the term "cast" when he said, *"Cast all your anxiety on Him because He cares for you."*

Here's what I found when I took a closer look. When Jesus instructed His disciples (including Peter) to "cast" their nets into the water, the Greek word is *ballo* – "to throw or let go of a thing without caring where it falls…uncertain about the result."[11]

But when Peter says to cast our cares on Jesus, he uses a different word – *epirrhipto*, which means "to throw upon or place upon,"[12] implying a certain result - an object to land on. It's used only one other time in the New Testament, when the disciples "cast" their garments onto the donkey on which Jesus would ride.

In 1 Peter 5:7, God isn't telling us to toss our worries and cares into the wind, not knowing where they will land. Instead, He invites us to cast them with certainty onto His broad shoulders. Why? Because He, the God of the universe, cares about us and has the wisdom and power to deal with those cares for us.

~

Today you're facing disappointment,
Fear, or pain, or loss.
God says, "Remember, child,
You can bring them to My cross

And let them there be crucified,
As you have been with me.
I'll take them from you there, and cast them
In the deepest sea."

Blessings in the Rain

Then as He lifts your burden,
You will find a sweet release,
As He replaces all your cares
With His abiding peace.
~

*[Jesus said,] "Come to me,
all you who are weary and burdened,
and I will give you rest."
Matthew 11:28 NIV*

~ Questions to Consider ~

What's bothering you today? What's causing you anxiety, fear, discouragement?

Have you cast that care from your own shoulders, onto Jesus? If not, why not?

~ Room for Reflection ~

Who can better handle your cares and anxieties, you or God?

Do you tend to try to deal with your problems on your own, first? Or are you quick to take them to Jesus?

~ *Day 78* ~
Yes, Lord, Let It Be…

"What do you want to be when you grow up?" "What will you do when you graduate?" "Are you going to get married some day?" Many of us heard these questions growing up. Many have asked them of others. Even as children, we think we know what we'd like to do, and sometimes even think we know how to make it happen.

There was a young lady in the Bible who probably had her life planned out, too. She would marry a godly man, be a godly wife, and raise godly children. They would be a respected family in their little town, and live happily ever after.

But then an angel came along and informed Mary that God had other plans that were going to blow hers out of the water. He would ask her to have a baby out of wedlock, which would ruin her reputation and possibly destroy her upcoming marriage. Something would even happen in the future that would "pierce" her own soul. (Luke 2:35).

As God dramatically changed her future plans, Mary willingly exchanged them for God's, to become the mother of the Savior of the world. Aren't you grateful that she did?!

~

"We can make our own plans,
but the Lord gives the right answer."
Proverbs 16:1 NLT

~

Sometimes I try to figure out
What God could use me for
Instead of simply asking Him
What plans He has in store.

Blessings in the Rain

My brain then takes off, traveling down
A straight, logical path,
Cuz I like things to just add up,
As if it's simple math.

But seems God likes to come along
With plans that blow my mind,
Reminding me that He works in
A different way and time.

He often asks for something more
Than I might think to do.
But when He does, I find He's there
To always see me through.

So I must learn, as Mary did,
To humbly say, "Okay.
Lord, let it be as You have said.
I yield to You this day."

And that's when God steps in to do
A wondrous work in me,
Simply because I answered, "Yes,"
To what God said would be.

~

"Mary responded, 'I am the Lord's servant.
May everything you have said about me come true.'"
Luke 1:38 NLT

~ Room for Reflection ~

If you had been in Mary's shoes, do you think you would've accepted
God's change in your plans as graciously as she did?

Has God ever stepped in with a major change in plans for you?

~ *Day 79* ~
Looking Back with Joy

"I look back on these last few months with joy.
I've never felt closer to God than I do right now."
- Beverly McKeone, Summer 2016

~

Beverly was called home to Heaven just a few weeks after sharing these thoughts. She battled her sickness bravely and graciously. And when Jesus said, "It's time," she was able to look back with joy - not because it felt good, for it did not. She instead found joy in the closeness and sweetness of her relationship with the One who would walk her Home.

I hope you know that same, sweet Savior. And that you, too, share the joy that can never be taken away.

~

I'm looking back with joy!

Not because the way has been easy;
for it has not.
Not because the pain diminished;
It did not.

But joy because my Savior walked with me,
holding my hand along the way.
He promised that He would;
and never let go.

Joy in finding Him a faithful Friend
who sticks closer than a brother;
and a good Shepherd who wades
through those murky waters
right along with me,
lifting me up on His sturdy shoulders
when it gets too deep,
or I grow too weary.

Blessings in the Rain

And joy in counting my many blessings -
the ones that made me smile;
and the harder blessings, too,
that took some time to see,
but were blessings, nonetheless;
blessings poured down on me
from my loving Heavenly Father
who works all things for my good.

And joy, at last, in the sweet anticipation
of seeing my Savior face to face.
Then I will know
it has been worth it all,
for He was always in control.

Yes, I'm looking back with joy.

And I'm looking ahead with joy, too…
Joy in spending forever and a day
with my precious Lord,
and someday, with all those I leave behind.

With Jesus, I truly count it all joy!
~

*"In all this you greatly rejoice, though now for a little while
you may have had to suffer grief in all kinds of trials.
These have come so that the proven genuineness of your faith —
of greater worth than gold, which perishes even though refined by fire—
may result in praise, glory and honor when Jesus Christ is revealed.
Though you have not seen him, you love him;
and even though you do not see him now, you believe in him
and are filled with an inexpressible and glorious joy."*
1 Peter 1:6-8 NIV

~ Room for Reflection ~

Can you look back on your life with joy?

~ *Day 80* ~
God, Be Merciful...

This poem is here especially for you... yes **you** - whoever is reading it today. I had not intended to include it. But at the last minute, I felt God nudging me to take another one out, and put this one in its place. I truly believe God chose each poem and the order of them for this book. But there's something special about this one being here. I may never find out who it was for. But if it's you, know that you were prayed for the day I put it in, May 6, 2020.

~

"The effective, fervent prayer
of a righteous man
avails much."
James 5:16 NKJV

~

My friend, you've struggled long into the night.
The burden that you carry is not light.
But when God doesn't take away the pain,
His Word says something greater will be gained –

A greater grace. A greater trust in Him.
A knowing, ever stronger, deep within
That He alone is there to carry you
When all else fails, when plans have fallen through.

For His plan never fails. Nor does His love.
His mercies new will bless you from above,
As slowly...ever slowly He unveils
The truth of how His goodness still prevails.

And in the morning, joy will surely come.
The night is long. Keep looking to the Son.

~

Blessings in the Rain

"God be merciful to us, and bless us;
and cause his face to shine upon us; Selah."
Psalm 67:1 NKJV

~ Room for Reflection ~

Do you have a friend in need of prayer? Did you know your prayers can be powerful and effective?

Think of those in your life, perhaps friends, family, fellow church members, teammates, roommates...anyone God brings to mind who is in need of prayer today. List them here; then take a moment to pray for them. Consider writing your prayer for them in the space below.

~ *Day 81* ~
Under His Wing

If you're looking for a place to hide today, a place of protection, peace, safety, shelter from the storm that's raging around you... there's no better place than this -

> *"The one who lives under the protection of the Most High*
> *dwells in the shadow of the Almighty.*
> *I will say concerning the Lord,*
> *who is my refuge and my fortress,*
> *my God in whom I trust:*
> *He himself will rescue you…*
> *He will cover you with his feathers;*
> *you will take refuge under his wings.*
> *His faithfulness will be a protective shield."*
> *Psalm 91:1-4 CSB*

~

Resting safely underneath the shadow of His wing,
I feel His strength surround me, and I need not fear a thing.
For when I'm tucked beneath His wing, I'm sheltered from the storm;
I'm lovingly protected as He keeps me safe and warm.

He may not take the storm away; the waters still may rise.
But if they do, I will not fear for love is in His eyes.
And I'm secure in knowing that my Savior loves me so.
He's promised that the trials I face today will never go

Beyond what, in His wisdom, He's determined I can bear.
He says that when I'm anxious I can come to Him in prayer
To leave my burdens at His feet, and rest in His embrace;
Assured that I am covered by His all-sufficient grace.

So though the storm may rage around me, I can be at peace
Because I have a God whose love and mercy never cease.
And time, and time again, He's proven true through everything.
There's no place that I'd rather be than underneath His wing.

"Be gracious to me, God, be gracious to me,
for I take refuge in you.
I will seek refuge in the shadow of your wings
until danger passes."
Psalm 57:1 CSB

~ Questions to Consider ~

What words or thoughts come to mind when you picture a mother bird hiding her chicks beneath her wings?

Do you feel those same things when you think about your relationship with God? Why or why not?

~ Room for Reflection ~

When you realize you need shelter and protection from the storms or enemies around you, what do you do first? Do you try to handle things yourself? Or are you quick to run to your Heavenly Father's side?

Are you cooperative when it comes to staying put in the shelter of God's wings? Or do you tend to be anxious to be free of the confines of His wing?

~ *Day 82* ~
How

Do you ever feel guilty about questioning God? Is it okay to ask Him why? and how? and when? and all those other questions swirling through your mind?

It's not like God is unaware of your thoughts. So voicing those thoughts isn't going to shock Him. In fact, He's your Abba… your Heavenly Father. If you have questions and concerns He wants you to bring them to Him. Just look at Job and David in the Old Testament. They didn't always get an answer. But that didn't stop them from pouring out their hearts to God.

So go right ahead. Tell Him what you're thinking today.

~

How do I live with joy and grace
When life is full of pain?
How do I reach that place where I
Can count my loss as gain?
How do I take unanswered prayer,
And see Your hand of mercy, there?
How can I fully live?
Where is the joy You give?

How do I live with joy and peace
When life just falls apart?
What do I do with shattered dreams,
Or a badly broken heart?
How do I know You really care
When I can't seem to find You there?
How can I fully live?
Where is the hope You give?

Blessings in the Rain

Look for the gifts, My child, and see
Even in times of pain,
Along with the trials you must endure
I sent blessings in the rain.
And when things start to fall apart,
Don't close your hands, your eyes…your heart.
For those are the times I give
More fully, that you might live.

And child, when it comes to unanswered prayer,
I answered My way, for I truly do care;
And wanted, for you, what was best.
Look closer, for you have been blessed.

~

*[Jesus said] "I have come that they may have life,
and have it to the full."
John 10:10 NIV*

~ Room for Reflection ~

Do you feel like you have that "life…to the full" that Jesus says He came to give you? Or does it feel like your life is more full of questions?

If you could see Jesus standing there with you today, do you feel like you could pour out your heart to Him, and ask Him about those things that are troubling you or breaking your heart? Why not do that now…

~ *Day 83* ~

For Grace, in the Hard Days

"Even when I walk
through the darkest valley...
you are close beside me."
Psalm 23:4a NLT

~

Knowing something is coming doesn't necessarily make it easier. But knowing the ONE who is coming helps.

The doctors had done everything they could. All that remained was for them to make him as comfortable as possible. And then he was gone... leaving Grace with an empty bed, and a broken heart. She had loved him well. But not nearly long enough.

It was in that darkest valley that she truly came to know the height, depth, and breadth of Jesus' love for her. And that His grace truly is sufficient. This was written for Grace, in the midst of those hard days.

~

Sometimes it washes over me again,
As teardrops fall unbidden like the rain
Just spilling down the same path as before.
I'm weary, Lord; and can't bear any more.

And yet, You ask just one more thing of me:
To open wide my eyes and heart to see
The wonder of Your love. Your hope. Your grace.
Here, even in this dark and lonely place.

And yes, the peace that makes no sense at all...
Oh Lord, I feel so helpless, weak, and small.
I need You so to take me by the hand,
To hold me gently, say You understand.

Then as You brush tears tenderly away,
I hear You whisper, "Child, trust Me this day.
My love for you flows fuller than your tears.
I'm right beside you. Feel Me draw you near."

And arms invisible, yet strong and sure,
Wrap tightly round. And I'm again secure,
Though still within this storm that I must face.
Here in its center, Lord, I've found Your grace.

And it's enough. For I have found it's true
That here I am held closer, Lord, to You.

~

*"Each time he said,
'My grace is all you need.'"*
2 Corinthians 12:9a NLT

~ Room for Reflection ~

What is the darkest valley you've had to walk through?

Did you have Jesus to walk through it with you? And if so, did you find that His grace was, indeed, enough to get you through?

~ *Day 84* ~
Stronger Faith than Fear

Cancer.

It never gets easier to hear. And never gets easier to say.

For Dan and me, it wasn't the first time sitting in a doctor's office, hearing that dreaded word. Cure or call to Heaven - both were possibilities, once again. The difference was we had learned by experience that Jesus would walk alongside us through whatever lay ahead.

So this time we recognized that the choice was ours... faith or fear.

In fact, every day, for each and every one of us regardless what we face, that same choice is ours. So, my friend, which will *you* choose today?

~

"You intended to harm me,
but God intended it all for good."
Genesis 50:20a NLT

~

There it is… that enemy is
Creeping in again.
But wait! Now I'm not sure if it
Is enemy or friend.

For that same thing that once struck terror
Deep within my heart,
That thing that Satan meant to tear
My faith in God apart -

I now recall the way God used
That very enemy
To draw me close, and stretch my faith.
It did not conquer me!

So raise your head again, my foe;
And see what God will do.
My faith is greater than my fear,
For God has seen me through!

And once again you'll see that what
You thought would bring me down,
Will simply add a gem to my
Faith-forged, grace-polished crown.
~

"Then you will experience God's peace,
which exceeds anything we can understand.
His peace will guard your hearts and minds
as you live in Christ Jesus."
Philippians 4:7 NLT

~ Questions to Consider ~

Is there an enemy currently in your life, threating to steal your peace and joy, trying to cause panic or fear, doubt or discouragement?

If so, is it an enemy you have faced before?

~ Room for Reflection ~

Have you seen God work on your behalf to change something that seemed like it was meant for your harm, but you now can see that God used it for your good? How did God turn it around?

~ Day 85 ~
Keep the Faith

Do you have those days when you can't help but wonder if God REALLY sees you? Does He truly know what's going on? Because if He did, surely He would do something. Please don't lose heart, my friend. God knows! He loves you. And He is already at work on your behalf.

~

"Why do you say... 'My way is hidden from the LORD;
my cause is disregarded by my God?'
Do you not know? Have you not heard?
The LORD is the everlasting God,
the Creator of the ends of the earth.
He will not grow tired or weary,
and his understanding no one can fathom.
...those who hope in the LORD will renew their strength.
They will soar on wings like eagles; they will run
and not grow weary, they will walk and not be faint."
Isaiah 40:27b-28, 31 NIV

~

Just because we have not seen
Fulfillment of the Father's plan
Does not mean we are any less
Held tightly, in His mighty hand.

For God is working outside time.
And He is not confined by space.
He will fulfill His promises
In His own time, at His own pace.

So do not be discouraged, friend;
Keep trusting His amazing love.
And know He's working all things out
As He's ordained in Heav'n above.

Then when we reach our Heavenly home,
And finally see things as we should,
We'll see the plans He had for us
Were always best, and for our good.

~

"being confident of this,
that he who began a good work in you will carry it on
to completion until the day of Christ Jesus."
Philippians 1:6 NIV

~ Questions to Consider ~

Are you "confident" that God is doing a good work in you, even today?

If not, what's shaking your confidence?

~ Room for Reflection ~

What might you do to regain your confidence in God's ability and desire to see His plan through in your life?

~ *Day 86* ~
Not by Sight

Peter, the disciple, walked on water. He actually stepped out of the boat and walked on water! As far as I know, he's the only one, other than Jesus, to do that. But many of us know the rest of the story, too. He took his eyes off Jesus, and began focusing on the wind and waves all around him; then began to sink. Good thing Jesus was there to take hold of his hand and rescue him.

And how easy is it for us to find ourselves in the same boat. We're walking along in our Christian faith, focused on God's Word and His leading; maybe even taking big steps of faith. But all of a sudden, storm clouds gather, waves start rising... and we take our eyes off of Jesus. Then just that fast, we too begin to sink into doubt, depression, and despair.

Jesus, Himself, reminded us (in Matthew 6) that if we would just focus on Him, He would take care of everything else. Why not give it a try?

~

"Set your mind on things above,
not on things on the earth."
Colossians 3:2 NKJV

~

Lord, help me set my heart above -
On things both pure, and true;
On mercy, grace, and loving well.
My eyes, Lord, fixed on You!

Then I won't be downhearted when
Things-earthy pass away,
For my heart will be seeking One
Who won't change day to day.

And that is blessed assurance when
Those storm clouds fill the skies,
When my ship tosses to and fro
As waves around me rise.

Blessings in the Rain

I'll lift my eyes from circumstance.
Oh please, Lord, hold me tight
So I can walk along with You,
By faith and not by sight.

~

"For we walk by faith,
not by sight."
2 Corinthians 5:7 NKJV

~ Questions to Consider ~

What circumstances around you today make it difficult to keep your eyes on Jesus?

What can you do to help keep your focus on Jesus, instead?

~ Room for Reflection ~

Can you recall a time in the past when circumstances got the better of you, and you allowed the cares of this world to crowd your thoughts, making you fearful or doubtful? If so, did you find yourself, as Peter did, being rescued by the hand of Jesus?

~ Space for Grace ~

Take a moment to thank Jesus for the times He has held out His hand to invite you to walk with Him on the water (taking big steps of faith). Then thank Him, too, for the times He held it out to rescue you when you began walking by sight, instead of faith.

~ *Day 87* ~
Part of the Process

[after 3 ½ years without rain]
"Elijah said to Ahab, '... there is the sound of a rainstorm.'
Then he said to his servant, 'Go up and look toward the sea.'
*So he went up, looked, and said, '**There's nothing**.'*
Seven times Elijah said, 'Go back.' On the seventh time, he reported,
'There's a cloud as small as a man's hand coming from the sea.'
Then Elijah said, 'Go and tell Ahab, 'Get your chariot ready and go down
so the rain doesn't stop you.' In a little while, the sky grew dark with
*clouds and wind, and **there was a downpour**. "*
1 Kings 18:41-45a HCSB
~

We've all experienced dry seasons in our lives – those times when we struggle to hear God's voice or see His moving in our lives. It seems there is little or no growth. And we become discouraged and maybe feel distant from God. But God has a purpose, even in those drier times. He may be testing our patience, stretching our faith. Whatever it is, trust that it won't be forever. Keep checking your horizon. God will send the rain again, just when it's needed most.

~

We've all seen times of blessing where
We're praising Jesus' name.
But what about those drier times
That come between the rains.

Those seasons, too, are sent by God
To stretch our growing faith,
To teach us perseverance and
Reliance on His grace.

It's all part of the process –
A foundation being lain;
A time to see God's faithfulness
Through times of doubt or pain.

Blessings in the Rain

Then when our hearts are driest,
If we'll still watch and pray,
A single cloud will signal
That rain is on the way.

And once again He'll pour out
His blessings, in due time.
The challenge, then, is patience knowing
His ways are not mine.

~

"See how the farmer waits for the precious fruit of the earth
and is patient with it until it receives the early and the late rains.
You also must be patient."
James 5:7-8a HCSB

~ Questions to Consider ~

What might be the cause of dry spells in our lives, either spiritually or
emotionally?

What can we do to encourage ourselves during those drier times?

~ Room for Reflection ~

If you can recall a dry time in your life, do you recall God teaching you
anything special during that time?

~ *Day 88* ~
Praying for a Miracle

"When he came near, Jesus asked him,
'What do you want me to do for you?'"
Luke 18:40b-41 NIV

~

Are you praying for a miracle? Something big, that only God can do? If not… why not? We have a God who can do BIG things! And if it's the best thing for you, He will surely say, "Yes!"

~

"He who did not spare his own Son,
but gave him up for us all—
how will he not also, along with him,
graciously give us all things?"
Romans 8:32 NIV

~

There are miracles of healing.
There are miracles of joy.
There are miracles of peace when Satan's
Plot was to destroy.

Sometimes God sends the miracle
That we had prayed we'd find.
But other times He sends us peace
To trust His way and time.

No matter what the miracle,
With God, we know we're blessed.
For it is His desire to give us
Only what is best.

So knowing that our God is love,
And gave for us His Son,
Means we can thank Him, even now,
Before the answers come.

Blessings in the Rain

" 'For I know the plans I have for you,' declares the Lord,
'plans to prosper you and not to harm you,
plans to give you hope and a future.'"
Jeremiah 29:11 NIV

~ Questions to Consider ~

Do you need a miracle in your life? Something big, that only God can do?
If so, what is it?

Have you asked God for that miracle?

~ Room for Reflection ~

If there is something you're hesitating to ask God to do or provide in your
life, why haven't you asked Him?

"If you, then, though you are evil,
know how to give good gifts to your children,
how much more will your Father in heaven
give good gifts to those who ask him!"
Matthew 7:11 NIV

~ *Day 89* ~
Spring Snow

As I sit here finishing up *Blessing in the Rain*, it's the middle of May and there's white stuff flying past my window. It's not giant rain drops, nor is it cottonwood seeds that sometimes gather like snowdrifts along the roadside. It is, in fact, SNOW! in May. in southern Pennsylvania.

When we lived in upstate New York, occasional snow squalls in May were rather expected, and somewhat accepted. But this is not New York. And this does not feel like Spring!

But whether or not it feels like Spring doesn't make it any less so. And whether we can see God at work doesn't make that any less so, either. Sometimes God asks us to believe regardless of how things look. That's called faith. And God calls it "reality" and "proof," no matter how things look or feel.

~

*"Now faith is the **reality** of what is hoped for,*
*the **proof** of what is not seen."*
Hebrews 11:1 HCSB

~

So… I'll choose joy, though it doesn't feel like spring.
There's snow upon the ground, but birds still sing;
For somehow in their hearts, they seem to know
That spring's still there, beneath the fallen snow.

No, I can't always go by what I feel.
Sometimes I've got to trust that what is real
Goes far beyond what I might touch or see;
That truth is not diminished one degree
By whether senses say that it is so.
Yes, it's still spring, regardless of the snow.

Blessings in the Rain

And some days it is hard to feel God's love.
He's promised me His blessings from above,
And that He'll work out all things for my good.
He wants for me to trust Him; and I should.
But on those days of struggling through the pain,
It's hard to feel the love fall with the rain.

That's when my hope and faith must rest upon
A love that's proven faithful, all along;
A love that runs so deep I somehow know
That God declares He loves me, and it's so.

~

"Blessed are those who have not seen and yet believe."
John 20:29b CSB

~ Questions to Consider ~

Do you FEEL like God loves you today?

What evidence do you have to prove that He does?

~ Room for Reflection ~

Have you ever wondered if God really loves you? What might make you question His love? And on the other hand, what might make you sure of it?

~ *Day 90* ~

We Receive Your Grace!

*" Indeed, we have all received
grace upon grace from his fullness,
John 1:16 HCSB*

~

"We receive Your grace!" These were the words of my friend, Gloria Spears, as she received a scriptural blessing from another friend. There's nothing quite like those moments when we've grown weary in battle, trying to carry a heavy load; then along comes a friend, or Jesus Himself, reminding us that we can lay those burdens at His feet, and lift up our newly emptied hands to receive the grace He offers in its place.

Are you ready to lay down that heavy load you've been carrying, and receive, instead, His amazing grace?

~

We lift up weary hands that have
Been toiling all day through.
We empty them of burdens as
We cast them, Lord, on You.
And we receive Your grace.

We lift up moistened hands that have
Been wiping tears away.
Those tears are in Your bottle; and
That's why our hearts can say
That we receive Your grace.

We lift up joyful hands, so full
Of blessings from above.
We give them back to You, Lord, as
A token of our love.
For we've received Your grace.

Thank You, Lord!

~

~ Room for Reflection ~

Rather than closing out our devotional journey together with more questions, I would instead like to leave you with a blessing. I pray this will encourage your heart as you continue seeking the face and grace of Jesus, embracing His many *Blessings in the Rain.*

"The Lord bless you
and keep you;
the Lord make his face
shine on you
and be gracious to you;
the Lord turn his face
toward you
and give you peace."

Numbers 6:24-26 NIV

Blessings in the Rain

Endnotes

1. Ann Voskamp. http://www.aholyexperience.com/2013/06/7-things-you-need-to-know-when-youre-overwhelmed-cant-keep-up/
2. Ibid
3. Beth Moore, *James: Mercy Triumphs.* (Nashville, TN, LifeWay Press, 2011), pg. 176. Duplicated and used by permission.
4. Anna B Warner, "Jesus Loves Me" in *The Hymnal for Worship & Celebration,* ed. Tom Fettke (Nashville, TN: Word Music, 1985), 579.
5. Ann Voskamp. http://www.aholyexperience.com/2014/09/because-the-world-is-dark-we-really-need-you-5-ways-to-keep-being-brave/
6. Jennifer Kennedy Dean, *Live A Praying Life* (Newhopepublishers.com), pg. 168.
7. Fanny Crosby, "He Hideth My Soul" in *The Hymnal for Worship & Celebration,* ed. Tom Fettke (Nashville, TN: Word Music, 1985), 496.
8. Anthony Loke. *Tears in a Bottle.* 2007. https://bit.ly/3bY9d5P (accessed April 29, 2020).
9. Gil Smart. *How a pastor's wife found blessings, and inspired others, while fighting cancer.* 2019. https://bit.ly/2Yyx8Vk (accessed May 2, 2020).
10. John Bartz. January 25, 2019. https://www.facebook.com/donna.bartz.3
11. Bible Study Tools. 2020. https://bit.ly/2W4ldNs (accessed May 5, 2020).
12. Ibid

Index of Scriptures

Blessings in the Rain

Index of Poems

Poem Title	Day

Blessings in the Rain

About the Author

Lisa (Kesinger) DeVinney was born in rural Indiana, in 1966; and raised in a Christian home. At the age of seven, she gave her heart to Jesus Christ.

When Lisa was twelve years old, her father answered God's call to full time ministry; so she and her siblings spent their teenage years as a pastor's kids in Skaneateles, New York.

Following high school, Lisa spent two years at Houghton College, majoring in Math and Education. And during that time, Lisa married her best friend, Dan, whom she'd known since sixth grade. At the end of that year, his job took them to western New York.

Over the next nine years, God blessed Dan and Lisa with six children: five boys, followed by a baby girl. Lisa stayed home with the kids as they moved from New York to North Carolina, and back again to New York. The kids all played sports through high school, and some in college. So Lisa spent lots of time as a sports mom, and loved every minute of it!

After their youngest child graduated from high school, God surprised Dan and Lisa with a call to full-time college ministry with the Fellowship of Christian Athletes. They are serving in southern Pennsylvania where Lisa has the opportunity to use her passions for teaching, baking, and photography to minister to students and coaches at Millersville University.

It is Lisa's desire and prayer that God would use these devotionals to draw hearts closer to Him. There is, after all, no greater pursuit in this life than that of a closer relationship with the one true God!

If you'd like to contact Lisa, you can most easily find her on Facebook at https://www.facebook.com/lisa.k.devinney.

Also by Lisa DeVinney

**Sunday School Lessons 2012 –
Followers of God, 3rd-6th Grade Level**

Great Men and Women of the Bible

**I Will Life Up Mine Eyes:
366 Daily Devotionals in Poetry and Scripture**

**Rivers in the Dessert:
366 Daily Devotions in Poetry and Scripture**

Giving Your Life to Jesus

The scriptures and poems in this book are full of encouragement and promises for those who call Jesus Christ their Lord and Savior. If you have never made that commitment and would like to, here's what you can do to start a personal relationship with God:

God loves you! and wants you to have a real, personal relationship with Him where you can talk to Him and hear from Him every day; and after this life, spend eternity in Heaven with Him.

"For this is how God loved the world: He gave his one and only Son, so that everyone who believes in him will not perish but have eternal life."
John 3:16 NLT

But you and I are sinners – that means we fall short of God's mark of perfection. We do things that are wrong, we ignore God, and we try to find our fulfillment, joy, and peace everywhere but in God. So **our sin and pride separate us from God**, and from experiencing His love and plan for our lives.

"For everyone has sinned; we all fall short of God's glorious standard."
Romans 3:23 NLT

"For the wages of sin is death, but the free gift of God is eternal life through Christ Jesus our Lord." Romans 6:23 NLT

The best news ever is that **Jesus made a way**! Our sin earned us a death sentence, eternal separation from God. But He came down from Heaven and died a cruel death on a cross to pay that penalty for us. The best part is He didn't stay dead… He came back to life showing us that He has power over both sin and death – the power to offer us forgiveness, grace (His underserved favor), and eternal life as a gift.

"But God showed his great love for us by sending Christ to die for us while we were still sinners." Romans 5:8 NLT

"Christ suffered for our sins once for all time. He never sinned, but he died for sinners to bring you safely home to God. He suffered physical death, but he was raised to life in the Spirit."

1 Peter 3:18 NLT

All that's left for us to do in order to have eternal life in Heaven, and a relationship with God now, while still on earth, is to **receive that amazing gift** He offers. We do that by acknowledging that we are indeed sinners, in need of a Savior; and that Jesus did what we could not – in His sinlessness, He paid our penalty in full when He died on the cross. God says

"If you openly declare that Jesus is Lord and believe in your heart that God raised him from the dead, you will be saved."

Romans 10:9 NLT

Declaring Jesus as Lord means we turn away from our sins, and surrender our hearts and lives to Him. God's desire is that we would love Him *"with all your heart, all your soul, and all your mind."* (Matthew 22:37)

The offer has been extended to you, and the choice is yours. Are you ready to receive God's gift of salvation through His Son Jesus? It's the best decision you'll ever make! He has great plans for you…

"God saved you by his grace when you believed. And you can't take credit for this; it is a gift from God. Salvation is not a reward for the good things we have done, so none of us can boast about it. For we are God's masterpiece. He has created us anew in Christ Jesus, so we can do the good things he planned for us long ago."

Ephesians 2:8-10 NLT

My prayer is that if you do not yet know Jesus as your Savior, that you will accept His gift of salvation this very day! If you do, there will be great rejoicing in Heaven, and I will see you there one day.